THE WHICH?
COMPUTER
TROUBLESHOOTER

WILL GARSIDE

BOOKS

CONSUMERS' ASSOCIATION

CONTENTS

INTRODUCTION

Since the first IBM PC went on sale in 1981, computing power has doubled almost every two years and the prices of hardware and software have fallen rapidly. The range of computer software has grown from word-processing programs through business tools such as spreadsheets, databases and presentation software to fast-paced action games rendered in stunning 3D with audio quality better than that of any hi-fi system. Nearly two decades after that first PC, almost every person in the UK now has access to a computer and the Internet through work, school or the ubiquitous Internet cafés springing up across the country.

Whatever our views on Microsoft's monopoly, its Windows operating system, used by 300 million people worldwide, is now the pivot of this PC revolution. The ability to use this software is considered essential by employers and educators alike.

When the PC is used to access the Internet the possibilities for both work and play increase immensely.

The Which? Computer Troubleshooter aims to solve the problems and answer the questions you may have in the course of using a PC. No technical knowledge on the part of the reader has been assumed, which is why the book takes care to set the scene for each topic before launching into troubleshooting mode. Often, after all, it is the simplest things that cause the greatest problems — and provoke the reaction 'If only I'd known that when I started!' on the part of the frustrated user.

This book offers simple explanations, useful tips and guidelines for more advanced troubleshooting. It demystifies computer terminology and devices, provides instructions for configuring software and hardware, and so on right through to advising on the repair and upgrading of your PC. Acronyms and other computer jargon are explained in the glossary (and often in the text as well), and the book is extensively cross-referenced. While no single book could cover every possible combination of hardware and software, for the most part this book deals with the scenarios faced by the majority of computer users and offers a method for finding out what has gone wrong.

This book focuses on Windows 98 owing to its popularity among home users. (Windows 2000, a newer version, is targeted at business users.) On the surface, Windows 2000 and Windows 98 are very similar, but the former offers extra features for mission-critical tasks such as data-centre applications and network operation. Users of Windows 95 will find that most of the features, tips and troubleshooting guides in this book are as relevant for them as they are for users of Windows 98. Where there are major differences, text has been added to assist users of both types of operating system.

What this book is not is a substitute for the user manuals that some PC manufacturers provide with their computer systems. However, only a few companies offer proper documentation and, sad to say, most of these manuals, apart from being written with the expert in mind, are far from comprehensive.

Of all the ways to learn about computers the one that some people find the most rewarding is informed trial and error. Like good car mechanics, electricians, plumbers and carpenters, many so-called computer experts are often self-taught. They were not born with a natural gift but they managed to get to grips with the basic principles and then experimented with hardware and software to solve problems or create their own ideal set-up.

With the help of *The Which? Computer Troubleshooter* and, no doubt, a little trial and error, we hope you will soon be in a similar position.

PC prices are constantly falling while technology makes state-of-the-art machines seemingly out of date within a few years. But buying a PC is all about finding a system within your budget that fits your needs. This section will help you to decide what type of PC, and printer, you should opt for, and suggests some questions to ask before buying.

WHAT DO YOU WANT TO DO WITH YOUR PC?

Mostly fast action games	Consoles such as Playstation, N64 and Dreamcast offer a comparatively cheap alternative to a PC	If you are set on a PC, look for a computer with a powerful graphics card with at least 16Mb of video RAM and 128Mb of system RAM

Design and graphics
Look for a system with a large hard-disk space as graphics tend to take up a lot of memory: 18Gb of hard-disk space and at least 128Mb of RAM. An Apple computer is a viable alternative because it is well suited to creative work

A bit of everything
Look for a PC with built-in applications such as MS Office, a modem and plenty of internal upgrade slots. You can normally find offers that include a printer, digital camera and scanner as well

Word processing and Internet access
You do not need a very powerful machine for word processing or Internet access. The latest browsers and word-processing packages require only a Pentium 75MHz CPU, 24Mb of RAM and less than 100Mb of hard-disk space to function. These are the minimum requirements, so performance will be sluggish but not unbearable. However, you should get a fast 56K modem for web access. A second-hand machine could be worth considering

Buying a scanner

In recent years scanners have become much more affordable. Before buying one, consider the speed at which each page is scanned and the type of connection it requires to work with your PC. Scanners using USB are often much quicker than parallel scanners. Some scanners are also built into printers. Often called multifunction devices, they offer scanning, printing, photocopying and faxing all in the same package. The advantages in saved desk space and cost often outweigh the limitations of only being able to do one task at a time.

Buying a second-hand PC

You can save a great deal of money, as you can with cars, when you buy a computer second-hand. Before doing so, consider the following points.

• Make sure that you get some kind of warranty with the system: 90 days parts and labour is pretty standard but make sure this also includes the software on the machine.

• Get a printed specification of the PC you intend to buy, with details of the make and model, including size of hard disk, amount of RAM, type and speed of processor, type of monitor and size of screen, and what software is included in the price. If the PC you receive does not match the written specification, you are entitled to a refund under the Sale of Goods Act.

• Be cautious of PCs that do not come with the operating system already installed. Getting driver software to make these older PCs work may be difficult, especially if the original manufacturer has gone out of business.

• Try to pay by credit card or cheque as this provides a paper trail in case the machine was once stolen. You can at least prove that you bought it from the seller.

• Always test a machine before buying. This should include the floppy drive, CD-ROM and display.

• Ask about possible upgrades. If you are told that the machine is 'not upgradable' be wary as it may not use standard parts, making future repairs or upgrades expensive or impossible.

Laptops

Although much more expensive than a comparable desktop PC, for people who travel a lot a laptop is a convenient alternative. But laptops are far less upgradable and upgrades tend to be more expensive. If a laptop is out of warranty, repairs can be costly. If buying a laptop new, enquire about extended warranties (e.g. two to four years).

CHOOSING A COLOUR PRINTER

| **Spots of colour for underlining or small images** | → | Standard bubble or inkjet operating at 600dpi resolution. The cost of the printer is very low but the cost per page is higher |

| **Full A4 colour including high-quality photographs** | → | More advanced inkjet printer with a resolution of 1200dpi and the ability to use special 'photographic' paper. These printers can take up to 10 minutes to produce one page in photo-quality mode. The cost of the printer is still quite low but the cost per page is higher |

| **Full A4 or larger colour produced very quickly** | → | Colour laser printers produce sharp images very quickly, in sizes up to A2, at a reasonably low price per page. However, the units are expensive to buy and to repair when out of warranty |

CHOOSING A MONO PRINTER

Mono laser printer
Available in various shapes and sizes. The key criteria are:
• PPM (pages per minute): from 6 (home) to 40 (industrial)
• DPI (dots per inch): from 300 (fine for text) up to 2,400 (crisp images)
• compatibility — which should include at least PCL5 or PostScript if you do a lot of DTP work

Buying a second-hand printer
Before buying a second-hand printer, check that the toner/ink cartridge is still available and that the printer driver software is included. Do a full print test using a PC, not just the built-in self-test

WARRANTIES

PC warranties have a language of their own. The jargon can be almost impenetrable and although after-sales service is a vital part of the purchase it can be difficult to know what you're getting. The three kinds of warranty are:

- 'onsite': the best type to have, because if there is a problem a computer engineer will visit your home or office to sort it out
- 'collect and return' (C&R), the next best type, under which the PC manufacturer will send a courier to collect the PC from you, then sort out the problem on its own premises. There is no charge for this — just the inconvenience of having to stay in twice for couriers
- 'return to base' (RTB): this has many similarities to C&R in that the PC must go back to the manufacturer for repair, but under this arrangement you must arrange and pay for the carriage.

As well as knowing what type of warranty you have, you should find out whether repairs are carried out within a guaranteed time period. Most onsite warranties pledge to have an engineer by your side the next working day (sometimes subject to the initial call being logged before a particular time), with faster service available for a price. If the PC has to go back for repair, most companies will endeavour to return it to you within a week or a fortnight. Including travelling time for the machine, this is reasonable. Although even the most respectable manufacturers may only guarantee a 28-day turnround time, this is simply to cover their backs. Any company which mutters about how long a repair will take and warns of typical turnrounds of four or six weeks is probably trying to play on your fears to sell you an extended warranty.

Whether it is worth paying more for onsite cover is up to you. Assuming a reasonably quick turnround, a return-to-base warranty is adequate for home users. All onsite cover gives you is convenience, but if you are running a business, onsite maintenance may be essential. Extending the standard one-year warranty given by the PC manufacturer to cover, say, three years' onsite cover should not cost much more than £100—£150; if you want a guaranteed response within a shorter period, such as four hours, it will be more expensive.

One thing to watch is the manufacturer's telephone helpline. Normally if you have a hardware problem you can call either a freephone or a local rate number – at worst, it should be a national rate call. However, software problems are a different matter. Manufacturers' software helplines tend to be on premium-rate numbers – they are expected to be self-funding. If you bought your software with the PC, you will have to phone the PC manufacturer for help, not the software developer. This is particularly important for programs such as Windows and Microsoft Office. If your copy of Windows came with your PC, Microsoft technical support staff won't talk to you directly.

What warranties cover
A warranty will normally cover only actual mechanical faults. If the problem

you are experiencing is caused by software configuration the PC manufacturer is unlikely to offer any help; it may instead redirect you to the software manufacturer's support line.

Buying system components from various suppliers often causes manufacturers to pass the responsibility for warranties to the others, which is a good reason for sticking to a single supplier. A single supplier is also more cost-effective if you need an extended or comprehensive warranty package.

Purchase protection

The first worry when buying a PC by mail order is whether it will arrive at all: it has been known for computer assembly companies to take a stack of orders, cash the cheques and then vanish with the money.

Fortunately, these cases are rare, though this is small comfort if you are unfortunate enough to be caught. However, protecting yourself is relatively easy. Most important is to buy from a reputable company. Magazine reviews can help here: companies which make a consistently good showing over a period of months are well worth shortlisting.

If possible, pay by credit card. The Consumer Credit Act ensures that the card issuer is jointly liable for any private purchase between £100 and £30,000: if your computer does not arrive, you will get your money back. In theory, this also makes the card issuer liable for any warranty problems that arise, though in practice you will find this more helpful in applying pressure to the manufacturer than in making it accept responsibility.

Note that this protection does not apply to credit cards first issued before 1971, to debit cards (e.g. Switch or Delta), to charge cards such as American Express, or to company purchases.

Although buying from a magazine advertisement carrying the Mail Order Protection Scheme logo may seem safe, do not rely on this. It is hedged with restrictions – for instance, your purchase may have to have been the exact model advertised in the magazine – and a strict cash limit ensures that few people can be recompensed in respect of any one advertiser.

Extended warranties

Be wary of extended warranties, which are often aggressively sold, over-priced, and unclear about what they offer.

Assuming that the standard warranty covers one year's onsite maintenance followed by another two years of return-to-base cover, you should expect an extension to three years' onsite to cost about £100. You may pay more if the standard warranty offers less in the first place. If you feel you are being given the 'hard sell', especially if the small print includes dire warnings about the shortcomings of the standard warranty, steer clear. The odds are that the salesman stands to earn a handsome commission if you sign up.

One of the main advantages of a desktop PC is its flexibility. The variety of software available is as important as the way in which Windows can be tailored to your individual needs. Throughout this guide you will find examples of menus and configuration screens taken from Microsoft Windows 98.

Although Windows 98 has a great deal of similarity to its older sibling, the ground-breaking Windows 95, it incorporates many improvements. Even with the launch of Windows 2000, Windows 98 is still the most popular operating system, with Windows 95 a close second. Windows 2000 has had a slow uptake among home users, partly because it has no major improvements over the 98 version. New PC buyers have the choice of Windows 98 for home users or Windows 2000 for business users.

For users of Windows 95, additional explanations or diagrams are provided where the differences between the two operating systems are significant, but in most cases the information in this book is pertinent to both Windows 95 and 98.

This chapter is designed to familiarise new users with the basic hardware and software elements of a modern desktop PC running the Windows operating system. Note that different PC manufacturers may pre-install Windows with different colour schemes, settings and supplementary programs. As the number of possible variations is huge, we have chosen the most common settings as a basis for explanations and troubleshooting.

Before you start upgrading or repairing your PC, it is essential that you familiarise yourself with the basic menus and settings covered in this chapter. However, remember that if you do make a mistake you are unlikely to cause your PC any permanent damage and making mistakes is sometimes the best way to learn.

INTRODUCING YOUR PC

THE PERSONAL COMPUTER

Cables and sockets

When a PC is being set up, usually the cables will fit only in one way, and with very little force. If you do get a cable in the wrong socket, the machine may not start up correctly but it is unlikely to cause any permanent damage.

For a personal computer (PC) to work it needs hardware and software. Hardware consists primarily of the screen, the system unit (main box), the keyboard and the mouse. Software comprises programs such as word-processing packages, databases and games. To operate both hardware and software you need to have an operating system — the most common of these is Windows 98. This section introduces you to the main parts of your computer system.

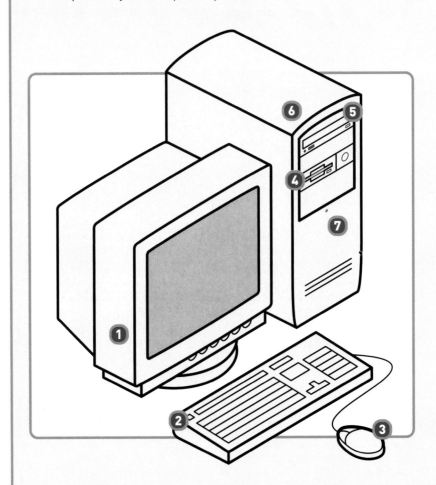

Warning!

As a safety precaution, you should never plug in or remove peripherals while the system is switched on.

1 **Display** Working on a similar principle to a television, the computer screen (also called the monitor or visual display unit) shows what the computer is doing.

2 **Keyboard** A PC keyboard has between 102 and 117 keys normally arranged in a similar way to a typewriter. It allows you to enter text and has special keys for controlling Windows (see section 1.4 for details).

Common peripherals

Speakers Computer speakers are similar to speakers used in hi-fi equipment, but they usually have a volume control dial built into the chassis.

Printers Printers come in many shapes and sizes. The main distinction is between ink-based and laser types. A further difference is that they can be colour or monochrome.

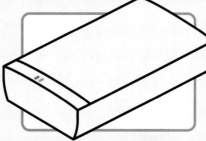

Scanners These devices make digital copies of paper-based images or text, which are transferred to the PC.

Control devices The most common device for controlling PC software is the mouse. For action games, however, a joystick (pictured here) is almost essential, while for graphics artists often use a tablet, which is a bit like an electronic sketch pad.

3 **Mouse** The mouse is the most common method of controlling Windows and software applications. Moving the mouse with either hand controls an on-screen pointer used for selecting items. See section 1.3 for details.

4 **Floppy drive** This is where you insert 3½-inch disks (which are not floppy). They are used mainly for moving information from one computer to another.

5 **CD-ROM drive** This is where you insert CD-ROMs, which store audio and visual information.

6 **The internal hard disk** This stores the Windows operating system, the software and files. It is hidden inside your PC. Most computers have a flashing light showing when they are in use.

7 **Power switch** The switch that turns the machine off and on (see section 1.2 for details of other switches).

Creating backups of Windows

When you first set up your PC, look for the CD-ROM with the original Windows operating system (OS) on it.

Some manufacturers do not give you the CD-ROM — instead, to save money, they place the OS files on the machine's hard disk. This means you must create a Windows back up set using up to 20 blank floppy disks.

This backup process is time-consuming but essential in case you need to re-install Windows.

In either case, make sure that the paperwork you have received includes a 'certificate of authenticity' with a Microsoft hologram on it, otherwise you will miss out on technical support and it may mean that you have an illegal copy of Windows.

BOXES AND LIGHTS

This section shows you what the different switches and lights on the computer signify and how to adjust the monitor.

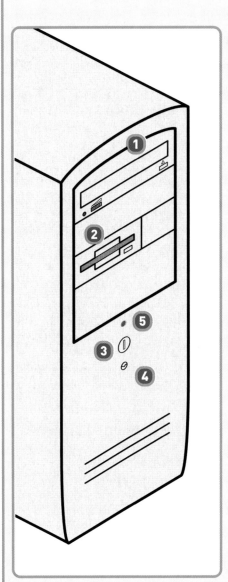

What's the difference between a CD-ROM drive and a DVD drive?

CD-ROM drives can play only music and computer software CDs. DVD (Digital Versatile Disk) drives can also play DVD disks – a newer type of disk used for videos, music and software.

1 CD-ROM or DVD drive
Computer or music CDs or DVDs are inserted here, on a sliding tray. Press the button to slide out the tray, and place the disk on the tray, label side up. Press the button again to load the disk into the computer.

2 Floppy disk slot
Floppy disks are used to store information. Push a disk into this slot, label side up, metal slide in first, until it clicks. To remove it, push the button next to the slot and the disk will pop out.

3 Power switch
This button turns on the power to your computer. Never use it to turn off the power, except in emergencies. Normally the 'Shut Down' feature (see section 1.6) is used instead.

4 Reset button
This is used as a last resort when your computer stops responding. It forces your computer to restart, rather like turning the power off and on again.

5 Hard disk light
This light flickers when the computer is sending information to and from its filing system.

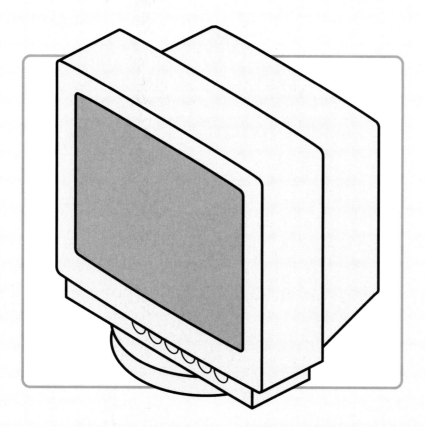

Monitors have controls that appear as finger-dials under the edge of the screen, or as buttons. You can sometimes improve the picture by changing these. If you have a more expensive monitor, these settings will be changed using an **on-screen display** (OSD). OSDs vary from one manufacturer to another and are generally similar to OSDs on television sets; they are usually very straightforward to use.

 Brightness
Adjusts the brightness

 Contrast
Adjusts the contrast

 Vertical position
Moves the picture up and down

 Vertical height
Controls the height of the picture

 Horizontal position
Moves the picture left and right

 Horizontal width
Controls the width of the picture

THE MOUSE

Types of mice

Many manufacturers produce a variety of mice. Ergonomic varieties can help reduce repetitive strain injury (RSI). Extra-high-resolution mice are commonly used for computer-aided design (CAD) and drawing applications.

The mouse is the most common way of accessing Windows. Moving the mouse with your hand makes a small pointer move on your screen. A mouse has either two or three buttons, each of which, when pressed, performs a different action on the item you have selected. The mouse can be used to manipulate files, control software and access the features of Windows.

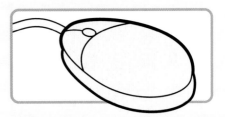

A typical mouse

Left button The left mouse button is used mainly for selecting an item. Note that a mouse for a left-handed person has the functions reversed.

Right button The right mouse button when clicked on an item normally brings up more information about the item and often additional menus for controlling the features of the selected item.

Centre button or wheel Some mice also have a centre button or wheel in between the left and right mouse buttons. This third controller often provides a short cut for scrolling a window up or down, while also acting as a trigger button in computer games.

Mouse cursor shapes and what they mean
The mouse regulates a cursor which changes shape depending on what your computer is doing or what item the mouse is resting on.

 This pointer is the most common type of mouse cursor and is used to select menus, files and options.

 You see this when you click on the help menu, select 'What's this?' and choose an item.

 The cursor looks like this if you try to select features in Windows that are not available.

 This hourglass symbol appears when Windows is busy doing something. You have to wait for the system to finish its task before doing anything else.

 The cursor turns into this shape when you have the option to select text, e.g. in a word-processing package.

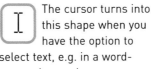 The cursor changes into one of these shapes when you move it to the edge of a window to change the size of folders or application windows.

 The cursor looks like this when you hold down the left mouse button on the edge of a folder so you can move it round the desktop.

 This signifies a link to a web page or another file.

Examples of mouse usage

Using the left click Clicking the left mouse button once generally selects a file, application or menu option

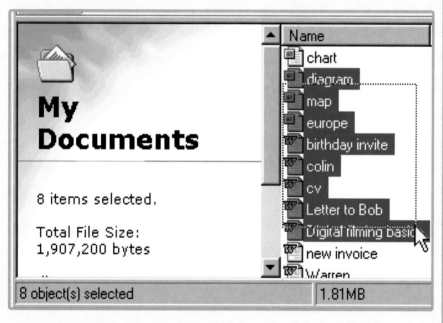

Double-clicking means clicking on an item twice in quick succession. This action on an icon opens the folder, runs the application or selects the menu option.

Holding down the left mouse button and moving the mouse allows you to select/highlight multiple files or menus that are adjacent to one another. If you want to select files or folders that are not next to one another, hold down the Ctrl key when holding down the left mouse button. You can then click the right mouse button and choose an option such as copy, cut or paste and apply that to the whole group you have selected.

Warning!

To prevent your mouse becoming dirty use a plastic mouse mat, which you should clean about once a month. Refer to the manufacturer's instructions on how to clean the ball and rollers of the mouse itself.

THE KEYBOARD

Keyboard essentials

A modern PC keyboard has about 102 keys. Most keys produce a letter, number or symbol when pressed. Generally, keyboards have several keys duplicated on both the left- and right-hand sides. Common keys that have a duplicate include Shift, Alt and Control (Ctrl).

The keyboard has two main uses — to type characters into software programs such as word processors or spreadsheets, and to access features of the software or change their settings. A computer keyboard is similar to a typewriter, but it has additional features. This section describes the functions of some of the most commonly used keys. Some keys, such as Alt, Tab, Insert, Page Up and Page Down, do different things in different applications.

1 Escape key (Esc) The Escape key has several different uses. In many applications Esc will end a program or cancel a task.

2 QWERTY keys The most popular type of keyboard starts with the letters Q, W, E, R, T and Y on the fourth row from the bottom. This is based on the arrangement of letters on a typewriter.

3 Punctuation marks and operators This group of keys includes punctuation marks and special symbols like @ and ~. The top ones are obtained by pressing the key while holding down the Shift key.

4 Return/Enter The Enter and Return keys are used to select an option from a menu or to move the cursor to a new line. They are generally interchangeable.

Warning!

Pressing keys on the keyboard while your PC is starting up can prevent the PC from starting up correctly.

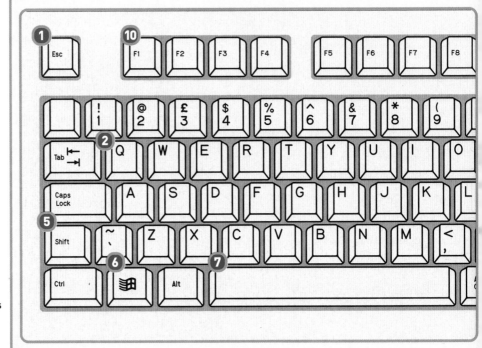

5 Caps Lock/Shift key The Shift key when held down while pressing another key produces an alternative character for the second key (e.g. pressing the 'Q' key normally produces 'q', but with the Shift key it produces 'Q' in upper case). The Caps Lock key when depressed allows you to type a number of characters in upper case.

6 Windows key When pressed, this key will bring up the main Windows Start menu.

7 Space bar When pressed, this bar produces a blank character in word-processing, spreadsheet and database applications.

8 Control key (Ctrl) This is often used in conjunction with another key to access a shortcut (e.g. holding down Ctrl while pressing 'B' creates bold text in most word-processing software).

9 Numeric keypad The numeric keypad allows quick entry of numbers. This is especially useful for data entry on to spreadsheets.

10 Function keys F1 to F12 Function keys often act as shortcuts to activate different parts of a program (e.g. F1 normally brings up on-screen help).

A keyboard to suit you

Several types of keyboards are available. In the UK and the USA the QWERTY typing system is the most common, although variations are used (e.g. in France the AZERTY system is preferred). Ergonomic keyboards help reduce strain on the wrists and hands of people who type for long periods.

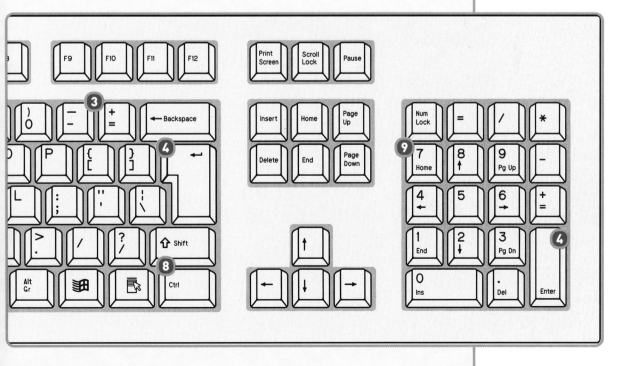

THE WINDOWS OPERATING SYSTEM

In the beginning...

The original Windows version 1.0 was first sold in 1985. The original eight-colour operating system was slow and littered with bugs.

Microsoft Windows is the most common operating system on home PCs. Windows provides an easy-to-learn interface for working with software (often called applications or programs) and hardware (often called devices or peripherals), and it comes with many useful programs to help you organise and customise your PC. Most of the Windows features can be accessed by using the mouse or the keyboard. This section describes the first Windows screen (called desktop) you see after your computer finishes running through a start-up sequence.

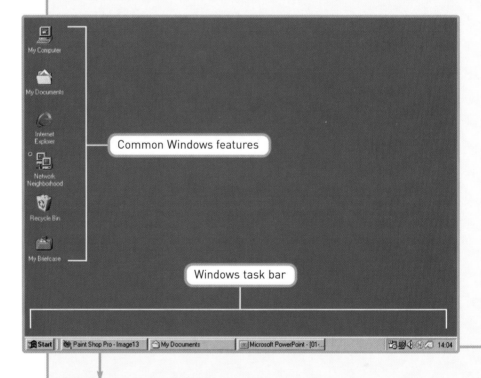

Common Windows features

Windows task bar

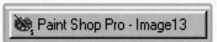

What are icons?

An icon is a picture that represents a link to software or documents. Double-clicking on an icon normally launches the program or opens up the document.

Applications These boxes represent applications which are currently running on the PC but which have been 'minimised' (removed from view). If you click on one, the application will expand to fill the whole screen.

Basic Windows icons

My Computer Clicking twice on this image (called an icon) allows you to explore your computer's hard and other disks. It lists the files and folders on your PC.

My Documents Many Windows applications store files such as letters created using word-processing software in this convenient folder. Clicking twice on this icon shows files stored here.

Internet Explorer Windows 98 comes with a built-in Internet browser. Clicking twice on this icon starts the Internet-browsing software and attempts to make a connection to the Internet.

Network Neighborhood Clicking on this icon lists the computers that are connected to your machine, either over the Internet or via a local area network. For most home users, this feature is not relevant.

Recycle Bin This is a special area of the computer that stores files that have been deleted. Clicking on it twice displays both the files that have been deleted and the options to restore them back into the system.

My Briefcase The briefcase is a way of transferring files from your PC to another computer via a removable disk.

Why is it called a desktop?

The main Windows interface is made to resemble a normal desktop. Like an ordinary working desk, the most commonly used items are close at hand. However, instead of drawers and pieces of paper, the computer uses electronic folders and files.

Free Windows tour guide

When you first start up Windows, you get the option to view an animated guide to Windows. Some installations of Windows may omit this tour but you can activate it manually by clicking on 'Start', pointing to 'Programs', then to 'Accessories', then 'System Tools', and then clicking on 'Welcome To Windows'.

14:04

Windows tasks The system applications row of icons, to be found on the bottom right of the screen, represents applications which are running in the background, automatically performing a useful function or controlling a system device — common examples include anti-virus checks, volume controls, printer drivers and multimedia players. Right-clicking or double left-clicking an icon generally launches a configuration program to allow you to change settings such as volume, print quality or virus-scanning frequency.

Double-clicking on the time function brings up a small calendar and options for setting time, date and geographical time zone.

THE WINDOWS DESKTOP

Differences in Windows 95 and 2000

The differences between the 95 and 98 versions of Windows are most noticeable in the interface screens. However, these variations are more cosmetic than anything else. Windows 95 users can, if they wish, upgrade their interface with a free active desktop add-on available from www.microsoft.com. Windows 2000 looks and feels very similar to the 98 version but it has some new features aimed at business users.

This section describes in detail the features of the Windows desktop. The Start button is a useful way to start software, manage information and control your computer. In keeping with the 'desktop' metaphor, Windows makes organising your work simple — instead of using filing cabinets or desk drawers to file away documents in appropriately named folders, you can create files and folders electronically.

Different kinds of icons

Every item in Windows has an icon. Icons normally represent what the item contains. The icon in this example is of a file called **'school report'**; if you double-click on it, a word-processing application will start and you will be able to see the school report on screen.

This next icon, called **'my work'**, looks like a loose-leaf folder and acts in a similar way. A folder stores other items and folders within it. Double-clicking on this folder icon will display the contents of the folder.

To make your desktop more convenient, you can create shortcuts to other files or software applications (e.g. by double-clicking on this icon called **'shortcut to database'** you can start a database application more quickly than by using the 'Start' menu). See section 2.6 on how to set up shortcuts.

How to organise folders

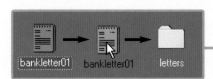

When you create a file, e.g. a letter to your bank, using word-processing software, you could name it 'bankletter01'. You could then choose to place it in a folder called 'letters', which has all your other letters in it. You could then create another folder

called 'personal' and put the 'letters' folder in it. In this example, the 'letters' folder is a sub-folder of the 'personal' folder.

The Windows 'Start' menu

The **'Program'** menu lists the software applications installed on the system. Older DOS programs may not always be listed here.

The **'Favorites'** menu lists folders created by the 'Add to favorite in your Internet browser' option (see section 7.2 for details).

Documents This option displays the most recently used files. Clicking on a file listed here launches the software that the file was created with.

Settings Advanced user settings are covered in section 1.11.

Find This is a useful tool for finding files on any drive attached to the computer. See section 2.9 for details.

Help The Windows help system can also be accessed by pressing F1.

The **'Run'** option is most commonly used for running older DOS programs and applications not listed on the 'Start' menu.

'Log off' will appear on this menu if

Help at hand

The built-in help system in Windows is usually accessed by pressing the F1 key. Leaving the mouse stationary over icons will often display additional help.

you have set up user profiles. If your computer is used by more than one person, user profiles allow each person's settings to be retained. See section 3.3 for details.

'Shut Down' allows Windows to be safely turned off. Remember to wait for the 'Safe to turn off' confirmation before switching off the power.

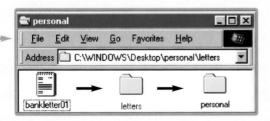

FEATURES OF APPLICATIONS

For you to perform tasks on the computer such as writing a letter, surfing the web or playing a game, your PC needs software (also called programs or applications). Applications can be started (run or executed) by Windows, using the mouse. This section explains some of the basic features of computer software. Section 1.8 deals with how to install new software on your machine.

WordPad – a typical software application

Toolbars Most software applications have a number of icons which allow you to access different functions quickly. In this word processor, you can change the font from Times New Roman by clicking once on the down-arrow icon to the right of the font description and choosing one of the options that comes up.

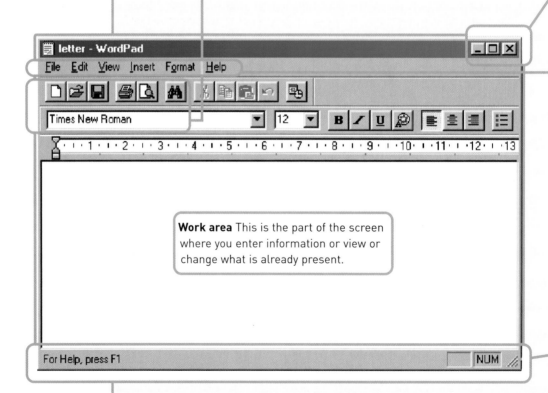

Work area This is the part of the screen where you enter information or view or change what is already present.

For Help, press F1   NUM

Control menu These three icons from left to right are used to minimise the window (which reduces the document to an icon on the Task bar at the bottom of the screen), maximise the window (so it takes up the full dimension of the screen) and close the application respectively. Most Windows applications have these control icons present.

Suite spot

Many software manufacturers group applications together in a suite, e.g. Microsoft Office, Lotus SmartSuite and Symantec Norton Utilities. The applications within them work similarly, so once you know how to use one, using the others is easy. Menus, icons and file formats often have the same style and mode of operation and some suites probe a centralised menu for changing features of applications within the suite.

'File' menu

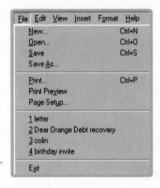

Most Windows software applications have a menu system (or a series of options) for accessing features of the program. Normally this starts with the 'File' menu.

The **'File'** menu normally contains options for you to create a new file, open an existing one or save one that is currently in use.

Most applications allow you to send their contents to a printer. Moreover, by using the **'Print Preview'** option you can see what the document will look like when it is printed.

The names of the last few documents that you worked on are shown here; as a shortcut you could click on one to open it up.

The **'File'** menu usually has an option to exit the software.

Information bar The bar at the bottom of many applications gives additional information regarding what features are currently selected or are available.

27

INSTALLING AND REMOVING APPLICATIONS

'Free' software

Some software manufacturers offer free versions of their product through the Internet or on disks mounted on the front of computer magazines. Many of these applications are old versions that have no technical support, and may come without certain key features. These demo packages are used to entice the user to purchase the full product and are often sold 'as is'.

Over 50,000 software applications are available to work with PCs running Windows. Some software will come with your PC, but you can add more to your computer by using disks (floppy or CD-ROM) or the Internet. Each piece of software usually comes with its own instructions for installing it on to your PC, but you have to be able to determine whether your machine has the right hardware and features for the new software to work correctly. Each computer has only a finite amount of resources, so you may have to remove older software to make way for newer software. You can install and remove software using Windows.

Installing software

The most common method for installing software is using a CD-ROM. Placing a disk containing software into the CD-ROM drive normally automatically installs the software. If the software fails to start, click on the **'My Computer'** icon and then on the CD-ROM to open up the main directory of the disk. This directory should contain a file called either **'Setup'** or **'Install'**; selecting one of these files normally loads the software on to your PC. See section 7.5 on downloading software from the Internet.

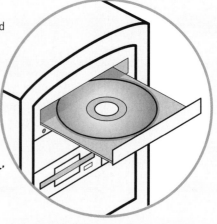

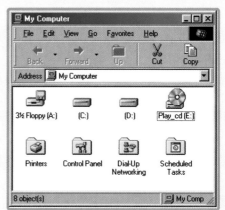

Removing software

Most new applications come with their own set-up and removal programs. These programs normally appear on the **'Start'** menu, directly under the application you wish to remove.

To install or remove one of the built-in Windows utility programs or older software applications, you need to go to the Windows Control Panel. To do this, click on **'Start'**, then select **'Settings'** and then click on the **'Control Panel'** option. The Control Panel contains numerous icons, each representing a different application. Find the **'Add/Remove Programs'** icon and double click on it.

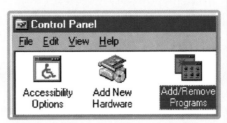

The **'Add/Remove Programs'** window has three main areas:

• **'Install/Uninstall'** This tab is often ignored because, as has been pointed out, most new applications tend to come with their own set-up and removal programs. Applications listed

in the scroll box can be removed from Windows using this option.

• **'Windows Setup'** This tab takes you to the window featured below, from where you can add and remove Windows built-in utility programs.

• **'Startup Disk'** This tab is covered in more depth in section 2.4. Essentially, this allows the creation of a disk to restart your machine after a severe Windows crash.

Keep your installation disks safe

Many software manufacturers treat the original CD-ROM installation disks they supply to users as a proof of authenticity to protect against piracy. In most cases, if your disk becomes damaged, you have to send it to the software vendor, who will supply a replacement for a nominal charge.

1 | Introducing your PC

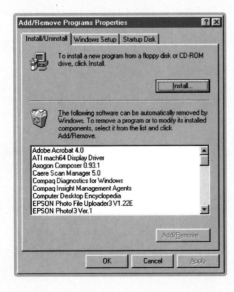

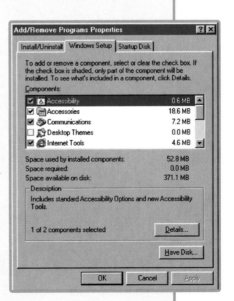

ADDING HARDWARE TO YOUR PC

The USB advantage

Universal Serial Bus (USB) is fast becoming the most popular way to connect peripherals to a PC. Its main advantages over the older serial and parallel ports are speed and connectivity. USB is about 100 times faster than a serial port and can have over 20 devices connected simultaneously.

Warning!

As a safety precaution, you should never plug in or remove peripherals while the system is switched on. The exception to this rule is USB, which is specifically designed for plugging in while the PC is still on (often referred to as 'hot swapping').

Various items of hardware, such as printers and scanners, can be attached to your computer to provide extra facilities. Each item, known as a peripheral or add-on, connects to your PC via a cable plugged into a socket at the rear of your machine. A peripheral requires software to allow Windows to control it. It may also have minimum requirements in terms of computer memory or processor speed, so before buying a new peripheral you need to check whether your PC can support it (that it is 'compatible' with the peripheral). Some peripherals are described in section 1.1; this section looks at other common ones and shows the sockets used to connect them. How to check on whether your PC is compatible with a peripheral is covered in the next section.

Common PC peripherals

Personal organisers Modern personal organisers or personal digital assistants (PDAs) work in harmony with PCs. If you connect your PDA to your PC (usually via the serial port), calendars and documents on both the machines can be synchronised, such that any changes on one will be automatically made on the other.

Digital camera The boom in digital photography has been fuelled by the huge potential cost savings over traditional chemical prints. Digital cameras hold pictures electronically and can transfer large amounts of data to the PC for editing. They often use the USB port for improved speed.

Projector A projector equipped with a compatible VGA (see opposite) port can be connected to your PC. Although it is quite expensive, it is useful for training purposes in offices, and also for certain games. A projector will plug directly into the display adapter of the PC graphics card.

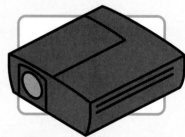

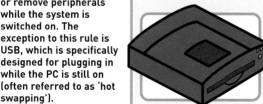

Backup tape/disk drive Hard disks can fail, sometimes rendering files unreadable. Low-cost removable tape and disk systems are commonly used to store copies of important files such as invoices, letters and accounts in case of hard-disk failure, error or even accidental deletion.

Interfaces for connecting PC peripherals

VGA/Display The VGA connector has 15 pins and is where the monitor is connected. Some advanced systems may have two of these sockets for dual screens.

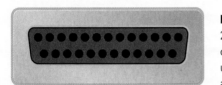

Parallel/LPT The parallel interface, a 25-pin connector, is generally used to connect the printer, but can also be used for scanners, tape backup units and a host of other peripherals.

With some computer peripherals you have a choice of whether to have an internal version (which resides within the chassis of the PC) or an external one. Often 'internal' devices have a speed advantage or a cost-saving.

Serial/COM The serial port is the oldest and most versatile connector for the PC. Often referred to as the communications port, it can also provide a low-speed connection between computers via either cables or modems. It can have 9 (as shown) or 25 holes.

Common examples of internal devices include tape backup units or CD-writers. When deciding on whether to buy an internal or external device, bear in mind that:

PS2/Mouse/Keyboard The PS2 socket is used mostly for keyboards and mice. Unfortunately, the sockets for both devices are identical and getting them mixed up is one of the most common technical support problems when users first set up new machines.

- internal devices can be more complicated to fit and may also need free spaces and appropriate mounting kits within the PC's chassis

USB Universal Serial Bus (USB) is a high-speed version of the serial port, and is standard on all new PCs. Because of its speed, USB is great for video devices, scanners and digital cameras.

- external devices can often be shared between multiple PCs and even laptops.

MIC/Line out/Speaker Essentially these ports are similar to headphone sockets and provide connections for audio devices such as microphones, speakers and amplifiers. PC manufacturers either colour-code or label each port to avoid confusion between the microphone and speaker sockets.

CHECKING YOUR PC's SPECIFICATIONS

When a peripheral, such as a printer, scanner or digital camera, is attached to your PC it makes demands on the machine in terms of memory, so you need to be sure that your PC has sufficient memory to support it. Also, how well a peripheral functions may depend on the speed of your computer. Most PCs are compatible with printers; new machines normally can support additional peripherals such as scanners and speakers. However, if you wish to attach a new peripheral to your machine you must check that your machine has the resources to support it.

Right-clicking on the **'My Computer'** icon (see section 1.3) and selecting **'Properties'** displays the main **'System Properties'** menu. This is probably the most important configuration screen and contains information about every piece of hardware and the majority of Windows system files on the machine.

The first tab is general information about the Windows software, including when it was installed and who the registered user is. The screen also gives details of the processor in the system and how much RAM is installed. It may contain information unique to the PC supplied by the manufacturer to help identify the machine during telephone support calls.

Specification sheet

When you buy a new PC, you will be provided with a specification sheet that lists the speed and type of the processor (e.g. 400MHz Intel Pentium II), the amount of RAM measured in megabytes (e.g. 64Mb) and the size of the hard-disk drive measured in gigabytes (e.g. 8.4Gb, which is 8,400Mb). The list will include the type of graphics card and the extra devices, such as modems and DVD drives, that come with your PC.

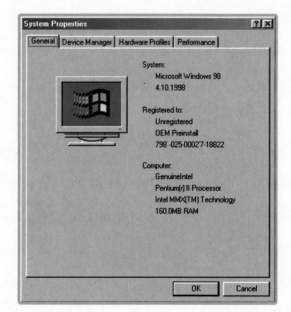

Device Manager

The **'Device Manager'**
tab lists all the devices
that Windows believes
are installed on the
system and also
whether each device
appears to be working.

Each device belongs
to a group, e.g. disk
drives or display
adapters; a group can
contain more than one
device. Clicking on the
+ symbol on the left of
a group lists all the
devices within that
group.

Right-clicking on a
device and selecting
Properties displays

more detailed
information and allows
you to change the

device's configuration.
This is covered in more
depth in section 5.7.

This is covered in more depth in section 5.7.

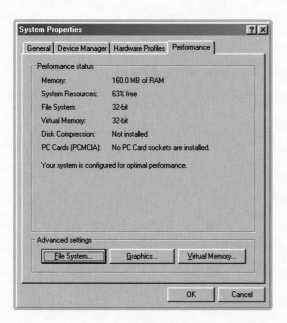

The **'Performance'** tab
gives more information
about the amount of
resources (RAM) and if any
disk compression (see
section 2.8) is running on
the system.

The more applications
you run simultaneously, the
more the percentage of
system resources free
starts to decrease. If it falls
beyond a certain point, the
computer begins to use the
hard disk as a type of slow
RAM and you will notice
disk activity start to
increase.

Identifying
the chip

You may find when you
click on the 'General'
tab of the 'System
Properties' screen that
the chip in your
machine is identified
wrongly — e.g. your
CPU may actually be
manufactured by AMD
but may be shown as
an Intel Pentium
processor. This is
because the
processors are so
similar that sometimes
Windows cannot
distinguish between
them.

Warning!

**Unless you are
constantly experiencing
problems with your hard
disk, you are advised
not to change settings
within the 'FileSystem'/
'Troubleshooting' menu
as this can cause
Windows to start up
incorrectly.**

1 | Introducing your PC

USEFUL WINDOWS UTILITIES

Windows 98 comes with many extra applications. Some of these programs are useful for customising the way you access the hardware and software on your PC. Other Windows programs help to fix problems or improve the performance of your system. Windows also contains an in-built help system that can answer many of the common questions of first-time users. Most pieces of software also come with help systems, which provide invaluable assistance.

  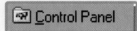

Clicking on **'Start'**, then on **'Settings'**, and then on **'Control Panel'** will bring up a screen similar to the one shown below. The functions of many of the utilities are explained below.

Add New Hardware

Adding new hardware is covered in sections 1.9 and 6.

Add/Remove Programs

Adding and removing software is covered in section 1.8.

Multimedia

Multimedia devices such as soundcards and midi-keyboards can be configured from here. These options are explored further in section 4.9.

Display

The changing display option is covered in section 3.2.

Installing and managing printers is covered in section 4.6.

Some features of the keyboard can be altered with this option. The speed at which characters start to repeat when a key is held down can be changed, as can the language you want to use. Keyboards with alternative character sets for Nordic, Turkish, Russian and a whole host of other languages are available.

The '**Fonts**' option allows you to display all the fonts on your system and add new ones. Fonts are available from software shops or the Internet.

This option allows you to set and change passwords on the system.

The '**Mouse**' option allows you to customise the mouse to suit your requirements.

Modems and faxing are covered in section 7.

'**Accessibility Options**' allows you to customise Windows to help users with visual or aural impairment. It also allows you to configure special devices such as one-handed keyboards or miniature joysticks to replace the standard keyboard and mouse respectively.

If more than one person is using the PC, the '**Users**' option allows you to set up the various users with their own passwords and display preferences. Section 3.3 covers this in detail.

With the 'Power' option you can specify how the computer behaves when left idle for too long. This includes automatically reducing the power to the screen and system unit after a period of inactivity (often known as 'going to sleep').

This option allows you to customise the sounds that accompany some common Windows tasks.

The '**Regional Settings**' and '**Date/Time**' options allow you to specify where in the world you are and the current time and date.

Warning!

Many Windows utilities contained within the Control Panel are used by other programs. Removing key applications such 'Dial up networking' may affect Internet and fax settings.

FREQUENTLY ASKED QUESTIONS

Most PC manufacturers provide instructions for setting up a PC for the first time. However, these can sometimes be confusing or not comprehensive enough. This section looks at the problems most commonly experienced by first-time computer users.

PRINTER PROBLEMS

The printer has power and paper but is still not printing. Why is this?
• Make sure the printer has an ink or toner cartridge installed. Check the printer manual's index under ink/toner/consumables for instruction on how to install consumables.
• Make sure the printer cable is firmly attached at both ends. Turn your PC off by clicking on the Start button at the bottom left-hand corner, then select **'Shut down'**. After your PC has shut down, turn the power back on and test the printer again. Do not use the **'Restart'** option, because only a full shutdown will send a reset command to the printer.

The printer is loaded with paper, so why, when I try to print, does the computer tell me that it is 'out of paper'?
• Try using fewer sheets of paper in the feeder.
• Many printers have two separate paper feeds, one for single sheets (often used for letterheads) and a main feeder for multiple sheets of paper. Try putting paper in both of these feeds and testing the printer again.

MOUSE PROBLEMS

Moving the mouse does not move the pointer on the screen. Why is this?
• The mouse and keyboard sockets often look very similar. Try swapping over the mouse and keyboard cables and restarting the PC.
• Some mice come with a protective shield. Turn the mouse upside-down and make sure that the mouse ball can spin freely. If not, open the bottom of the mouse to inspect it, and remove any fluff or dirt that is obstructing the ball.
• Some types of mouse use the serial ports (see section 1.9). Systems normally have two of these ports. Try the mouse in each port, restarting the PC each time.

SOUND PROBLEMS

The speakers are connected to the base unit, so why is no sound coming from my PC?
- Some computer speakers, unlike hi-fi speakers, have a separate on/off switch and volume controls. Make sure that these are correctly set.
- Some speakers need a separate power supply or even batteries: check that you have powered your speakers correctly.
- The PC has up to 3 audio sockets: one for speakers: one for a microphone and an additional socket for line-out. Test the speakers in each socket as these are often unlabelled. It is very easy to plug speakers into the wrong socket accidentally.
- Test your speakers with a Walkman to make sure they haven't blown.
- Make sure that the Windows volume control is set correctly. You can activate this control by clicking on the small speaker icon in the bottom right-hand corner of your desktop.

SCREEN/MONITOR PROBLEMS

There is power going to both my PC and the computer monitor, but nothing appears. Why?
- Try adjusting the brightness and contrast controls on the front of your monitor.
- Make sure that the cable between your PC system unit and the monitor is firmly attached, then restart your PC.

Part of the Windows desktop is running off the edge of the monitor. Why?
- The controls at the front of your monitor allow you to alter the position of the Windows screen in relation to your monitor's centre. Refer to the manual which accompanied your monitor, under **'resize/controls'**. Section 1.2 may also be of help.

WINDOWS PROBLEMS

My monitor, keyboard and mouse are all connected but Windows still won't start. Why?
- Make sure that there is no floppy disk in the floppy drive when starting the PC.
- Windows may fail to start if the keyboard or mouse are in the wrong port (the mouse and keyboard sockets are often identical). Try swapping them around and then restarting your PC.
- Make sure that none of the keys is jammed in the **'down'** position when you turn on the PC.

GENERAL TIPS

- Always keep all the manuals and software with the PC.
- Most companies which sell PC systems offer free technical support over the phone. Turn to your supplier first of all if you have problems in setting up your PC.
- If your PC appears to be totally dead, test the power sockets you are using for your PC with a lamp or alarm clock.

The modern desktop PC is surprisingly self-reliant. The operating system makes regular checks on hardware and software to make sure they are working, while smart applications send information on their status whenever they are used. If a problem does occur, Windows will try to fix it, or prompt the user towards remedial action. Unfortunately, things still do go wrong. Just as cars need regular servicing to keep them running efficiently, computer systems also appreciate preventive care. The housekeeping chores should take only a few minutes each week, but if you do them you will not only become more comfortable with your computer's functions — you will also speed up your system's performance. This section also explains the basics of how a computer system works.

HOUSEKEEPING AND QUICK FIXES

2.1 Inside the computer
PC technology fundamentals.

2.2 Looking after your hard disk
The hard disk, like a car engine, needs regular
servicing: this section explains how.

2.3 Files and their properties
A computer has millions of files. This section
explains what files are and how they work.

2.4 Creating backups
It is essential to make copies of important files, in case
your computer crashes. This section explains how.

2.5 Viruses and how to avoid them
An explanation of computer viruses and how to protect
your PC from them.

2.6 Moving information between applications
Cutting, copying and pasting information
between applications.

2.7 Deleting files
How to delete files and restore deleted files.

2.8 Disk compression
How to squeeze more files on to your hard disk by
means of disk compression.

2.9 Finding files
How to find files on your PC.

2.10 The Windows Startup group
About the programs that run automatically
when your PC starts.

INSIDE THE COMPUTER

Giving your system a boost

Although computer manufacturers constantly promote the CPU's speed as an indication of the performance of a computer system, RAM memory and graphics chipsets play an equally important part.

You can often increase the performance of a sluggish machine by simply adding more memory as opposed to buying a new system.

Warning!

Most PC manufacturers accept that users will want to upgrade their PCs at some point. However, some vendors withdraw technical support or warranties on systems they deem have been 'tampered' with. Always read accompanying material before opening a PC case.

Every activity performed by a computer can be broken down into three steps: the computer system receives information (input), it performs a task normally using software (process), and then produces a result (output). In the case of writing a letter, the input is your words keyed into the word-processing document; the process is the word processor arranging your text and running a spellcheck; and the output is your finished document or letter emerging from your printer. It is important to understand how different parts of a PC work together to perform a task, especially if you want to customise, upgrade or repair your machine.

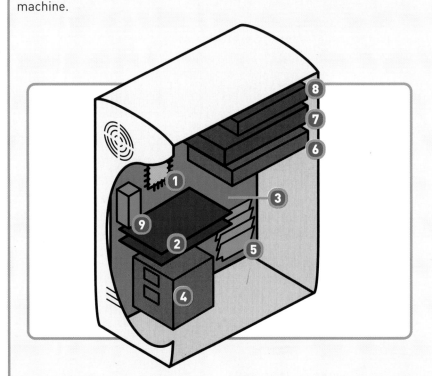

1 Central processing unit (CPU) or processor This chip is the heart of the computer, providing processing power for software applications. The CPU's manufacturer, compatibility type and speed rating (in megahertz) are printed on it.

2 PCI/ISA expansion slots
Most of a PC's flexibility is provided

by these slots. New PCs generally have at least two slots free for a variety of upgrade cards. Common upgrades include graphics, modems, network cards and soundcards.

3 Motherboard
The components of this logic board include the CPU and other chips, memory and expansion slots, and a

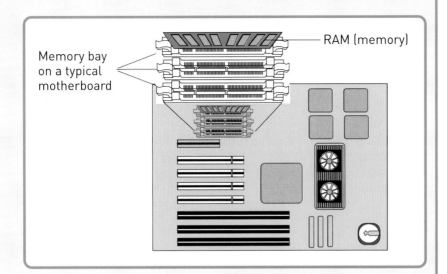

Memory bay on a typical motherboard

RAM (memory)

battery. Newer motherboards can support faster CPUs and more memory.

4 Power supply unit (PSU)

The PSU is a transformer which converts 230v mains into 5v and 12v used by the motherboard and internal devices such as hard- and floppy-disk drives.

5 Memory

PC memory comes in a number of shapes and sizes. The most common types are called DIMMs (Dual Inline Memory Modules) and come in 8, 16, 32, 128 or 256Mb sticks. Memory is used to run applications and store Windows settings. Without continuous power the contents of this memory are lost, which is why you must save your documents.

6 3¹/₂-inch 'floppy' drive

Although by today's standards the capacity of the 3¹/₂-inch disk drive is small at 1.44Mb, a disk is exceptionally useful for moving small documents between machines and is essential for restarting Windows after a system failure (see section 2.4).

7 CD-ROM drive

Although most systems still come with the read-only version of the CD drive, the trend is moving towards CD read-and-write drives. Each CD can hold 450 floppy disks' worth of information. It can also contain music, video and audio clips. Unfortunately, such CDs are quite slow compared with hard disks (but are considerably cheaper). See section 2.4.

8 Hard-disk drive

The hard-disk drive stores the operating system, the software and data a PC requires to run applications. The drive uses a platter of magnetic disks and a set of read-and-write heads to move information to and from the computer at up to 30Mb per second. The hard disk is resistant to shocks and dirt, but may wear out after about five years' use.

9 Interfaces

Many of the computer's interfaces, such as connections for the keyboard, printer and mouse, are built into the motherboard as standard.

Turning your PC off

It is a myth that computers need to be turned off when not in use. PC systems are designed to be left on permanently and when idle will automatically cut down on the power they draw. However, it is advisable to switch off the monitor, as it uses a lot of energy.

Taking your PC abroad

Most PSUs can handle different electricity supply systems. If taking your PC to another country, check that the PSU can handle the electricity supply there before plugging it in. This applies to the monitor and printer too.

LOOKING AFTER YOUR HARD DISK

The hard disk of your PC holds software, information about the hardware connected to the machine and the documents you have created. The disk can hold millions of bits of information and so looking after it is essential. Windows 98 provides software to manage the contents of your hard disk — especially to 'repair' files and organise the data on the disk to improve the performance of the system.

Maintenance options

To maximise the performance of a hard disk, you need to maintain it properly. Windows manages this task automatically for the most part, but you can choose to do it yourself. Click on the **'My Computer'** icon, then right-click on the icon of the hard drive, and select **'Properties'** and then **'Tools'** to bring up the maintenance options.

Scandisk

The error-checking program (ScanDisk) looks for corrupted files on the drive and either repairs them or allows you to delete them. This program has two main options, a standard check and a more thorough inspection. Although the latter takes longer, it can spot potential problems — e.g. it can alert users to parts of the drive that may become corrupted.

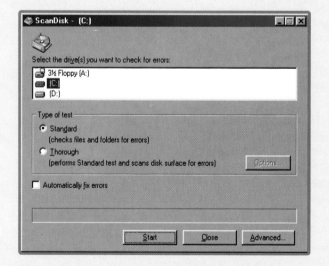

Warning!

Before starting a scan or defragmentation, make sure you have closed down all applications. This will improve the speed of the scan and the defrag, and prevent the applications from conflicting with the files used by these two programs.

These areas are marked as **'bad'** and are not used by the system for saving files, thereby preventing future file corruption.

Defragmentation

The **'Defragmentation'** option reorganises the files on the drive to make them load more quickly. It may not affect the file-loading speed noticeably, but it is useful if you have deleted a large number of files or have lots of small files on the system.

Both the ScanDisk and Defragmentation software can be automatically activated at times when the system is not in use. You can use the **Task Scheduler** (see section 3.5) to run them according to a schedule you specify.

File corruption

Like old vinyl records getting scratched or audiotapes becoming crackly, files can become corrupted through daily usage. On modern computers, file corruption is quite rare. However, viruses or an interruption in power supply could cause corruption.

Prevention is better than cure

Disk scanning and defragmentation should be done regularly — i.e. do not wait till a file becomes corrupt or a drive disorganised to do so. On average you should run the programs once a month; if you create and delete a lot of files each week, you should scan and defrag weekly.

FILES AND THEIR PROPERTIES

Your computer hard disk contains thousands of files. Each of these files is used by the software on your machine or by Windows to perform a task. Files may also contain information created by you, e.g. in the form of a letter or a spreadsheet. It is important to know what files you have on your PC and which programs can access each type of file. This section shows you where to look to find this information.

Properties of files

Each file, folder and application normally has an associated properties file, which conveys important information about the item and when it was created. To access an item's properties, right-click on its name and left-click on **'Properties'**. Some programs run configuration programs instead of showing file properties. These configuration programs allow you to change the settings of an application, much like the options on a menu bar. If you do not want to change any option, just click on an empty part of the desktop.

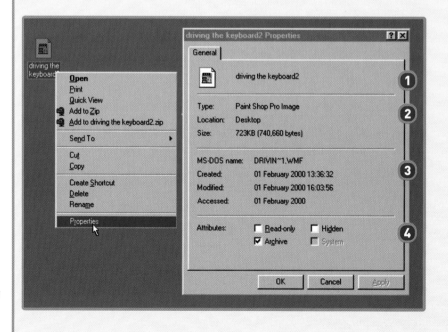

Warning!

Many file types work only with specific software. Trying to read them in other applications such as a word processor may produce gibberish.

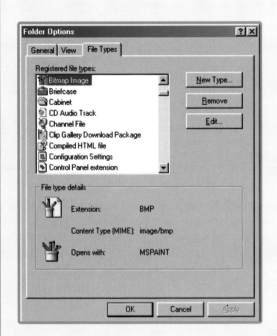

Types of files

Open up any folder and select **'View'**, then **'Folder Options'** and then the **'File Types'** tab. This brings up a list of file types and the programs that work with them.

1 This describes the file or folder name and can be up to 256 characters in length.

2 The file type is the most important property. It shows which applications can use this file type. Many file types can be used by more than one application. For a complete list of file types and their common usage, see the section at the end of the book.

3 The main part of the MS-DOS filename can be only eight characters in length, so for longer names the first six characters plus the ~ symbol are shown, followed by a number in case of duplicates. The three-letter extension or file-type descriptor indicates what type of file it is. In this case, WMF signifies a Windows Meta File, which is a type of graphic image often used in clip-art programs.

4 The attributes function allows you to alter the properties of a file. Read-only files give additional warnings if you try to delete them, archive files are used in conjunction with backup devices, while hidden files are not shown in directory displays but remain on the hard disk.

CREATING BACKUPS

PC systems nowadays are much more reliable than the first home computers which appeared in the 1980s. Unfortunately, they still break down from time to time. If your system does break down (or 'crash'), it will often repair itself, but valuable information may be lost. To prevent this from happening, it is essential to create and maintain backups. A backup is in effect a duplicate. It may contain information that Windows needs to repair itself or important documents that you cannot afford to lose. Windows 98 comes with some backup software but you need additional hardware and software to protect all the information on your system.

Creating a start-up disk

If Windows fails to start up correctly, a start-up disk can be used to boot the system up so that repairs can be made to corrupted files or Windows settings. The first step in creating a start-up disk is to click on the **'Start'** button, then select **'Settings'**, then **'Control Panel'** and then double-click on the **Add/Remove Programs Properties'** icon.

2 | Housekeeping and quick fixes

Types of backup

There are two types of backup you need to make. The first is backups of data files that contain information such as text or pictures; these should be made on a regular basis.

The second kind is a system backup (i.e. of the Windows operating system and applications); you should make this when you first get your system and before you go in for any major hardware or software upgrades (see section 1.1).

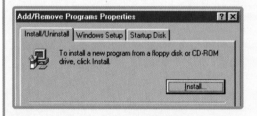

Next, click on the **'Startup Disk'** tab.

Make sure you have a blank 3$\frac{1}{2}$-inch floppy disk handy, then click on the **'Create Disk'** button. The system now asks you to insert the disk, which it will erase before copying across the key files needed to start Windows after a problem.

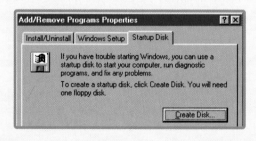

Types of backup device

CD-ROMs that can be 'written to' are becoming increasingly popular for backing up files of all types. Blank CD disks cost about £1 each and store up to 650Mb of information, the equivalent of 450 floppy disks. Unfortunately, such CDs are quite slow to use. Moreover, a single CD-ROM cannot hold all the information needed to back up a complete computer system, unlike magnetic tapes (see below). Disks that can be written more than once are now available.

Floppy disks are the easiest and cheapest method of backing up small files, and are commonly used for transporting information between computers. Each floppy disk holds 1.44Mb of information (the equivalent of several word-processed documents or images).

One of the oldest methods of storing computer data is the **magnetic tape**. Tape backup units vary in size from those that can back up all the information on a single computer to high-capacity units that can back up a whole network of PCs. Tapes are quite slow in operation but very cost-effective. A tape drive can be used for home PCs. It can be attached to the system via the USB or parallel ports (see section 1.9) or fitted internally like a floppy drive.

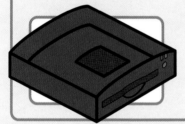

Removable disk devices such as the ZIP drive, HIFD and LS120 work in a similar way to floppy disks, but have a much greater capacity. Unlike floppy disks, however, different manufacturers' products are not compatible with one another. The cost of the disks is much higher than for tape or CD-ROM, but they can be written to many times.

When Windows has finished creating the start-up disk, remove the disk from the drive. To test the disk, close all Windows applications and shut the system down normally.

After the machine is completely off, place the start-up disk in the drive and turn the power back on again. The system will restart, but with DOS instead of the Windows desktop. (Disk Operating System, or DOS, is a text-based command language that was commonly used in the days before Windows and is useful for repairing Windows or for extracting important files when Windows is unable to start correctly.

For more on DOS, consult section 5.8.)

To return to Windows, remove the start-up disk and store it in a safe place. Next, turn off the power to your system, wait ten seconds, then turn the system back on again. Windows should now restart.

VIRUSES AND HOW TO AVOID THEM

Computer viruses are malicious programs that can potentially damage your PC software and occasionally parts of the hardware too. Although no software can guarantee 100 per cent protection against these programs, you can protect yourself by following the simple steps outlined below.

Virus outbreaks

Computer viruses are a serious threat. Even though the majority of viruses are not meant to be harmful, they can still cause problems with applications and computer devices. The most lethal viruses can wipe out the contents of your hard disk and in extreme (and fortunately very rare) cases, permanently damage your PC system.

The term **'computer virus'** is quite broad in meaning. The two main categories of viruses are self-replicating viruses and Trojans (malicious code).

The most common types of self-replicating viruses are associated with applications such as Microsoft Word and many popular email packages. Using a special type of programming language, these **'macro'** viruses try to attach themselves to emails or documents so that they can spread.

Trojans are less common. They are named after the Trojan horse of Greek mythology because they are programs that are disguised in an attempt to fool users into allowing them on to their systems. One example from the late 1990s was a program purporting to 'analyse your personality', and available for download from a number of adult-orientated newsgroups on the Internet. Once installed on an individual's PC, the software tried to erase the hard disk. These types of Trojan are rare but still crop up, especially in the form of DOS programs which can circumvent some Windows-based anti-virus software.

Viruses are a threat to even the best-prepared. In the summer of 1999, an outbreak of a new type of virus called Melissa even forced Microsoft to shut down its mail services for several hours while the infection was treated. In May 2000 the so-called Love Bug virus wrought havoc on computer systems across the world.

Windows has no built-in anti-virus software. This is because, unlike applications, anti-virus software needs to be constantly updated to be able to cope with new viral strains. Dedicated anti-virus specialists, who find viruses and produce antidotes, supply regular updates. You can find such updates on the Internet (see list of useful web sites at the end of the book) or you can have them sent to you on a disk for a monthly fee.

Ticking bomb . . .

Many viruses come with a 'payload'. This means that they get activated under certain circumstances (e.g. on a particular date or when the hard disk has reached a certain capacity), and then proceed to perform a harmful action such as wiping the disk. Unfortunately, prevention is the only cure.

The solution

Virus-protection software is neither 100 per cent effective nor free. The most common practice for manufacturers of such software is to give it away or include it with a new PC and then require the user to pay a monthly subscription for updates and customer support.

The various brands of anti-virus software are similar in terms of price and performance and are available from most computer stores or via the Internet (anti-virus web sites are included in the list at the end of this book).

You can protect yourself to some degree (for free) by following these simple steps.

- Avoid downloading EXE files from web sites you are not familiar with or if the manufacturer of the software is unknown. Trojan programs often have no documentation with them and require you to perform unusual tasks (such as booting from a clean disk) before installation.

- The most common types of virus use a simple programming language also used to write macros (commands set up to perform a series of actions). If you do not use macros within applications such as Word or Excel, turn this feature off from within the program's options to prevent macro viruses. To turn off a macro, press F1 within an application to list the help files. In these help files search for 'Macro' and follow the on-screen guidance.

- Be wary of unsolicited email which comes with either EXE or DOC files as these can contain viruses. If you receive such an email, check with the sender that he or she has sent it intentionally before you open up the attachment. Infected computers can often send out mail without the user knowing.

- Some free anti-virus shareware products are available. The most notable of these is FPROT, which has been around since 1982. For home PC users, this software is free and is available from http://www.complex.is/f-prot/. However, technical support is limited and updates are available only via the web.

- Be wary of software that is not on original disks or comes without boxes or manuals. This suggests that the software is pirated (illegal) and could contain viruses.

- Never leave a floppy disk in the drive when you power the system down. Viruses can live in the boot sector of the disk and can infect your system when it is next started up. This method of infection often leaves anti-virus systems powerless as the virus is already in memory before the anti-virus software has a chance to load up.

MOVING INFORMATION BETWEEN APPLICATIONS

In a computer system, all information is held digitally, as a series of ones and zeros which can represent text, numbers or even graphics. Using software called a clipboard, information can be moved between applications — e.g. a picture created in the Windows Paintbrush program can be copied and placed inside a word processor. This concept is common to most Windows applications and allows you to create multimedia documents by combining data from several applications.

Copying information

Most applications have a selection tool that helps you choose an item. In the Windows Paint package this selection tool is represented by a square with dashes. To select an area of the picture, click on this tool, hold down the left mouse button and select a part of the picture by moving the mouse. In the example shown below, the house and very little of the plain background behind it have been selected.

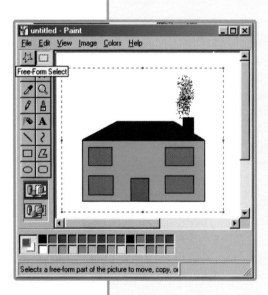
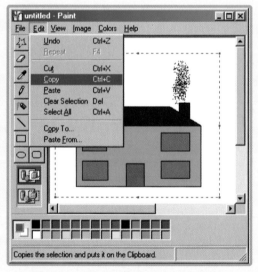

After making your selection, go to the **'Edit'** option and select **'Copy'**. The portion of the picture you have selected is now held in the computer's memory and can be placed in another application.

Pasting information

If you now go into another application, the Windows WordPad in this example, selecting the **'Edit'** menu and selecting **'Paste'** pastes the previously copied information into your document.

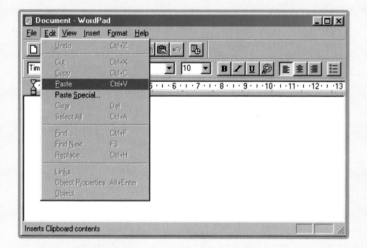

This type of cutting and pasting can be done between many different applications.

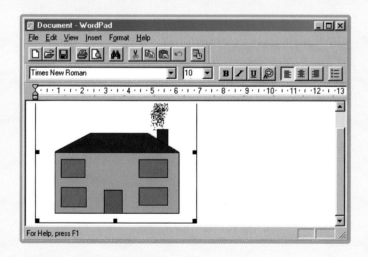

Speed tip

In many applications you can use a combination of keystrokes instead of the mouse — e.g. Ctrl + C to copy a selected portion and Ctrl + V to paste a previously copied item.

Creating shortcuts

You can use the 'Copy' command to create shortcuts on your desktop. First, select the item for which you want to create the shortcut, e.g. an application. Copy the item either from the file menu within an application or by right-clicking on the file and selecting copy. Next, select a blank area on the desktop and right-click to bring up another menu. Now select the 'Paste shortcut' option to create a new icon. You can rename this shortcut by right-clicking on the file and selecting the 'Rename' option.

DELETING FILES

Computer systems can hold billions of pieces of information within files and folders. However, the amount of space on a computer hard disk is not unlimited. Files need to be deleted to make way for new information or placed in special storage areas so they take up less space on the hard disk. Windows has special programs to allow files that have been accidentally deleted to be recovered and to maximise the amount of space available on the hard disk.

How to delete files

To delete a file, right-click on its icon and select the **'Delete'** option. Alternatively, you can select the file and press the **'Delete'** key. Deleting a file removes it from its current location and places it in the Recycle Bin.

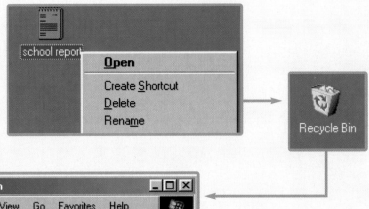

The **'Recycle Bin'** is a special area of the hard disk which stores deleted files. The location of the file before it was deleted is also stored in the bin. You can open the Recycle Bin and look at files that have been deleted. To remove files from the Recycle Bin permanently, click on the **'File'** option and select **'Empty Recycle Bin'**.

Freeing up disk space

If you want to free up wasted space on your hard disk, use the **'Disk Cleanup'** utility. To access it, click on the **'Start'** menu, then select **'Programs'**, **'Accessories'**, **'System Tools'** and then the **'Disk Cleanup'** option.

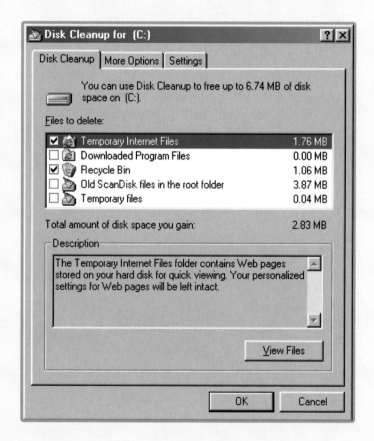

Select the areas you want to clean up and then click **'OK'**.

Other ways to delete files

You can delete files from within the load-and-save option found on the file menu of many applications. Select a file from within these menus and press the 'delete' key. Note that deleting files in this way may remove your option to retrieve them via the Recycle Bin.

How to retrieve a deleted file

Provided you have not already emptied the Recycle Bin, you can retrieve a file you have deleted by opening up the bin, right-clicking on the relevant file icon and choosing 'Restore'. This will result in the file being placed back in the directory you deleted it from.

DISK COMPRESSION

When to compress

Generally, compression needs to be run only once for a user to notice a big difference to the amount of hard-disk space saved. If, however, you delete or move a large number of files around, running the compression agent once a month may be a good idea.

Compression is not a quick fix when the drive is completely full, because to run the utility you need to have at least as much free space on the drive as is already used up.

Compression is a way of maximising the free space on your hard disk by making the files on the system smaller. In doing so, however, it reduces the speed of the computer. Windows has built-in tools for compressing files on your hard disk.

Compressing a hard drive

To compress your hard drive to accept more information you need to run the **'Compression'** utility, which can be found by clicking on **'Start'**, then **'Programs'**, **'Accessories'** and **'System Tools'**.

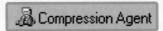

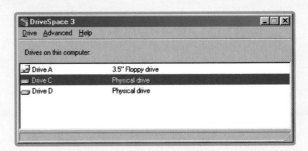

To compress a drive, select a drive, click on the **'Drive'** menu option then select **'Compress'**. The utility will start automatically if your computer supports compression (contact your PC's manufacturer if the machine does not support disk compression and you want it to).

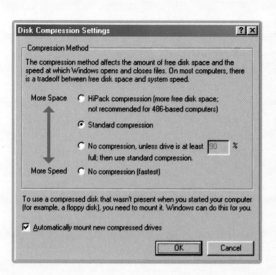

You then have to choose a compression method; the more compression you use, the slower disk performance will be. However, on a modern PC, choosing even the highest settings will result in very negligible slow-down.

How much free space is left on the hard-disk drive?

To find out how much space you have left on your computer's hard disk, double-click on the 'My Computer' icon, then right-click on the appropriate drive and select 'Properties'. This can tell you how much free space is available and also has a useful pie chart — a graphic representation of the amount of space left on the drive.

Examining a compressed disk

Once a drive has been compressed, you can examine how much space you have gained. To examine a compressed drive, right-click on the drive icon and select **'Properties'**. Now select the **'Compression'** tab to see the descriptive diagram pictured right.

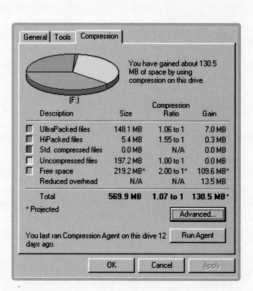

FINDING FILES

Given the amount of information generally stored on a computer, it is very easy to mislay an important file or folder. Even though files and folders have unique names, looking for them on a computer system containing millions of files and folders can be a daunting task. However, by using the **'Find'** facility in Windows, you can search for files of a certain type or which contain a specific word or phrase.

Understanding the 'Find' utility

The **'Find'** utility is located on the main **'Start'** menu. If you have an active Internet connection, you can also start Internet searches via this menu.

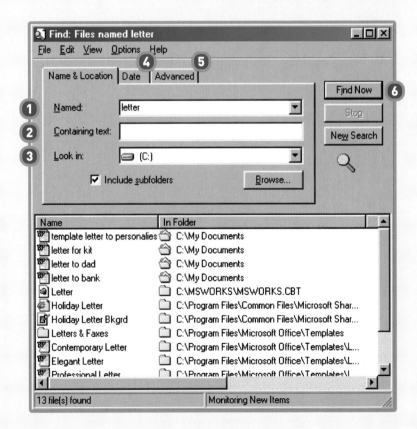

Warning!

Some files are hidden from the user by Windows. These may appear in grey in the search box; they are files used by the system and should not be altered in any way.

Using wildcards for more powerful searching

When filling in the name of the file or the file type you are looking for, instead of using whole words you can specify parts of words or groups of files. Below are examples of several types of 'wildcards'.

*.DOC   This option will list all files with the .DOC extension created by Microsoft Word.

WIN.*   This will list all files which have the letters WIN in any part of the name. The final * indicates that all types of file should be listed.

S?N.*   The '?' used in this wildcard means that the character between the 'S' and the 'N' can be anything. So any file names with the words 'sun', 'sin', 'son', etc. will be listed with this search.

Creating virtual folders

You can create your own 'virtual folders' by saving the results of a search. First perform your required search and then select 'File', followed by 'Save search'. A folder will be created on the desktop which will display shortcuts to all the relevant files.

1 In the **'Named'** box you can type in part or all of the file name you are looking for. In the example illustrated, typing in **'letter'** and clicking on the **'Find Now'** button will list any file with the word 'letter' in its name. Make sure that the **'Include subfolders'** option is ticked for the search to take place across the whole hard disk.

2 If you type a word or phrase in the **'Containing text'** box, the facility will look for a match within the documents it is searching for. If the previous example is modified to look for the word 'john' in the text, the software will look inside each file that satisfies the first criterion (i.e. the word 'letter' in the name) for the word 'john' and then display only those files which match both criteria. However, some file formats, such as spreadsheets and pictures, may have text within them that is compressed such that the text is not searchable. The **'Containing text'** option works best with word-processing files.

3 You need to specify where to look for particular files or folders. This option allows you to change starting drives or folders.

4 Using the **'Date'** option, you can specify that the software should look only for files which were created or modified within a certain range of dates.

5 The **'Advanced'** option can be used to specify files of a particular type (documents, pictures, spreadsheets, etc.) or of a certain size measured in kilobytes.

6 When you click on the **'Find Now'** button, the search criteria specified in steps 1-5 are put into action. The **'Find'** utility will display matches in the scroll box occupying the lower half of the window. Double left-clicking on a file or folder displayed in the scroll box will allow you to access it as normal.

THE WINDOWS STARTUP GROUP

When you turn on your PC, Windows performs many functions to test and set up both itself and the hardware which makes up your system. Many of these tasks are hidden and are part of the initial start-up process (often referred to as boot-up or booting). Some of these activities start programs such as anti-virus software, calendar and clock running in the background. You can change or add to many of these StartUp programs.

What do the StartUp icons mean?

The StartUp row of icons (see left) represents applications that are running in the background, automatically performing a useful function or controlling a system device. Common tasks include anti-virus checks, volume controls, printer driver and multimedia player. Each of these icons is unique to a different software manufacturer, but holding the mouse over an icon without pressing any buttons generally gives you more information about each one (see section 1.6 for details).

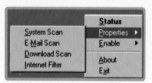

Right-clicking on an icon on the task bar often brings up options for the associated software. In this example, right-clicking on the anti-virus software icon allows you to start various types of scans.

A typical StartUp application

Double-clicking on the time function brings up a small calendar and options for setting time, date and geographical time zone.

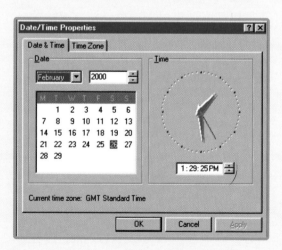

2 | Housekeeping and quick fixes

Altering the StartUp group

To access the StartUp folder, right-
click on the **'Start'** menu button and
select the **'Explore from here'**
option. After the Windows Explorer
pops up, select the **'Programs'**
folder, then the **'StartUp'** group.

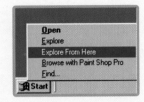

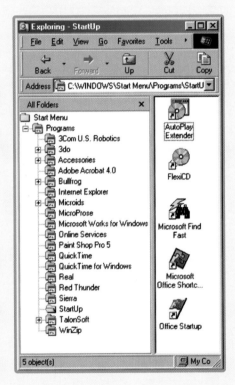

The StartUp group
displays the icons of
programs that are run
when your PC is booted
up. You can delete or
add files to this group
by using the standard
Windows cut, copy,
delete or paste
shortcut options
described in section
2.6.

For your actions to take
effect you will need to
restart your PC.

Warning!

If a program within the
StartUp group is
preventing Windows from
starting up properly,
restart the machine in
safe mode (see section
5.5) and then remove the
program. This could
happen when, say, a
device in the StartUp
group looks for a piece of
hardware that has been
removed, e.g. a scanner.

Every PC user has different requirements. Although some applications such as word processing and surfing the Internet are very common, arranging the computer's interface to suit your needs and your style can help your productivity. Windows has been designed to be highly capable of customisation.

Changes you can make range from simple (altering colour schemes, say) to complex, such as making Windows perform many tasks automatically. Users who started with Windows 95 may even want to remove some of Windows 98's fancier features to help them get off the ground more quickly.

Customising your machine will help to familiarise you with Windows operations. Experimenting with menus and settings will not damage your system, although it is possible that some types of customisation could cause Windows to behave in a strange and disconcerting manner, even if no error has occurred.

Before beginning any radical customisation, make a note of any of the settings you intend to tinker with. If the worst happens, just reset the settings to their original values.

CUSTOMISING YOUR PC

3.1 **Customising the desktop**
The desktop is highly adaptable to your individual
requirements, as this section explains.

3.2 **Screen properties**
How to set your computer monitor to different resolutions.

3.3 **Multiple users**
Managing multiple users on a single PC.

3.4 **Active Desktop**
Many web features can be incorporated directly on your
desktop, as this section shows.

3.5 **Scheduling activities**
Customising when and how tasks are performed, using
the Windows scheduler.

3.6 **Hardware profiles**
How laptops and heavily customised PCs can benefit from
multiple configuration profiles.

3.7 **Disk caching**
A method of improving PC performance.

3.8 **Power management**
How to reduce your PC's energy consumption.

3.9 **Windows Schemes**
Changing colours, fonts and sound using the
'Windows Schemes' utility.

3.10 **Accessibility options**
Features for visually and aurally impaired PC-users.

3.11 **Making your PC kid-safe**
Tips for setting up your PC so that children can use it, with
Internet safeguards.

CUSTOMISING THE DESKTOP

The Windows 98 desktop is the main interface for accessing features of your PC. It consists of icons (see section 1.5), which represent links to software or documents. Many aspects of the desktop can be personalised (or 'customised'). The preferences you can make range from the simple (e.g. changing colour schemes) to the complex (e.g. modifying how and where icons are displayed). This section explains how to customise your desktop.

Icons

By pressing the right mouse button over an icon or folder and holding it down, you can drag the item to anywhere on the screen. Make sure that the **'Auto Arrange'** feature (see right) is turned off, otherwise Windows will move the icons to where it believes they should be.

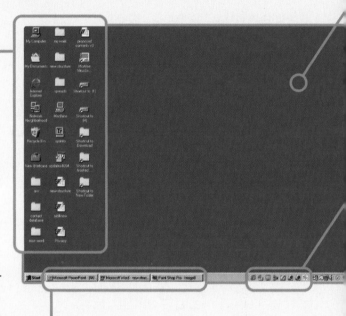

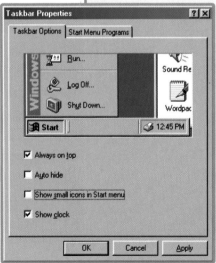

Taskbar properties

Right-click on the edge of the Taskbar to change how it behaves in Windows.

'Always on top' always places the Taskbar in front of any running software.

'Auto hide' removes the Taskbar if an application is running, giving more space to

the application.

'Show small icons' reduces the size of icons on the Taskbar.

'Show clock' shows the real-time clock.

The **'Start Menu Programs'** option is covered in more depth in section 1.6

Arranging icons

The icons on the desktop can be arranged in many different ways. Right-click on the desktop and select **'Arrange Icons'**. From this menu option, you can arrange the icons by name, type, size or date. The **'Auto Arrange'** function allows Windows to control how icons are displayed.

Options for the toolbar

The toolbar can be permanently displayed along with Windows applications. This area (like the **'Start'** menu) acts as a convenient way of accessing commonly used features. Right-click on the edge of the toolbar to change what is displayed on this menu and to add extra items.

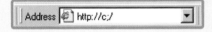

Select the **'Address'** option to give you a browser-like prompt such that if you type in a web page address, Windows will automatically try to connect to the Internet and go to that page.

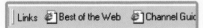

With the **'Links'** option enabled, any web site address added to the **'Favorites'** shortcut within the browser (see section 7.2) will be displayed along the toolbar.

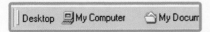

With the **'Desktop'** option enabled, every item on the desktop will be

replicated in a bar that can scroll from left to right along the toolbar.

With the **'Quick Launch'** option enabled, any kind of shortcut on the desktop can be moved to the toolbar so that it is always visible. To do this, right-click and hold on the item you want to insert, then drag it to the toolbar and release it. New icons will appear which can scroll from left to right along the toolbar.

More customisation

Each of the different elements of the toolbar, such as 'Address', 'Links', 'Desktop' and 'Quick Launch', can be moved around the toolbar and resized. In fact, the toolbar itself can be resized and moved to different positions around the screen. To resize an element, hold down the left mouse button on an element's description, e.g. the 'Links' button, and move it around. If you hold it on the edge you can resize the item, and if you hold it in the middle you can move it. The same is true of the toolbar itself. Play around with the desktop to see how much you can — and want to — customise it.

SCREEN PROPERTIES

A PC monitor is more adaptable than a television screen in that you can vary many of its features, including the image size and colour capacity. Depending on what kind of task you are performing, you can customise how your monitor displays items — e.g. if you are working with graphics, you can increase the resolution and colour depth. This section explains some of the screen properties you can customise.

High resolution
1,280 dots across
1,024 dots down

The resolution of the screen — i.e. how many dots across and how many dots down can be displayed at any one time — increases with the size of the screen. This resolution figure also includes an indication of the maximum number of colours each dot can display.

These two screens show the difference between high- and low-resolution modes. The high-resolution screen (top) allows more information to be displayed, and with much more detail and richness of colour, than the low-resolution one (below). On the screen below, very little of each application can be seen, and the colours look odd. Having at least 4Mb of memory on your graphics card and a large screen (17 inches or over) enables you to obtain a high-resolution screen.

Low resolution
640 dots across
480 dots down
256 colours

Changing screen properties

To change the features of your screen, right-click in the Windows desktop area and select **'Properties'**.

1 The **'Background'** tab allows you to select different pictures for your desktop background.

2 The **'Screen Saver'** tab allows you to set up a colour screen saver that will start automatically if your PC is left unattended for long.

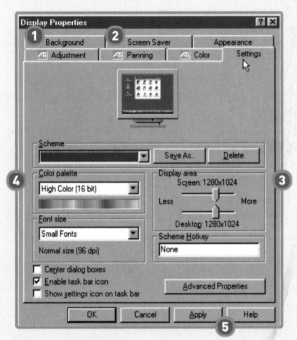

3 The two **'Display area'** sliders affect the resolution of the screen and also how much is displayed at any one time. You can have e.g. a desktop of 1,280 x 1,024 but set your screen size to 800 x 600. With these settings, when the mouse reaches the edge of the visible area the screen scrolls to show the rest of the desktop. This feature is sometimes used in conjunction with large fonts to help visually impaired users.

4 The **'Color palette'** can be varied between 8 bit (256 colours) and 24 bit (16 million) colours. The former is sometimes used with older programs or to improve the PC's performance (the fewer colours it has to manipulate the better it performs),

while the latter is preferred for work with graphics or the manipulation of photographic images.

5 The **'Apply'** button activates any setting you have changed within the **'Display Properties'** section.

Jargon watch

Computer screens have many different names, including monitor, cathode ray tube (CRT), visual display unit (VDU) and display. The most common display for PCs is the super video graphics adapter (SVGA) standard. SVGA monitors range in size from 14 to 21 inches (measured diagonally).

Speed tip

Some PCs use system memory rather than the graphics card to hold the screen image. On these systems, reducing the screen resolution or colour depth can speed up the performance of applications and games.

3 | Customising your PC

Screen savers

The screen saver was created to stop monitors burning out when they displayed the same static image for a long period of time (when the the computer was left unused for a while). This problem has been eliminated by modern monitor design, but a screen saver is still useful as a security measure — set up such that when it is on a password is needed to re-enter the Windows desktop.

You can specify the period of inactivity after which your screen saver should come on, and can choose from the options on Windows or personalise it by, say, having news headlines downloaded from the Internet.

MULTIPLE USERS

It is quite common to find a single PC being used by an entire household. In such a situation, each member of the family may have their own preferences on how they want the machine to look and feel. By using the 'Multiple Users' option, each user can customise the computer's features for him- or herself.

To enable Windows 98 to support multiple users, you must first open up the 'Control Panel' and double-click on the **'Users'** icon. The first time you do this, the Multi-user Setup Wizard will run (see right).

The wizard first asks you for a username. This is the name you have to type in when you log in to the computer.

You then get prompted for a password, which is optional. If you choose to have one, you must enter it twice just to make sure you entered it correctly the first time.

3 | Customising your PC

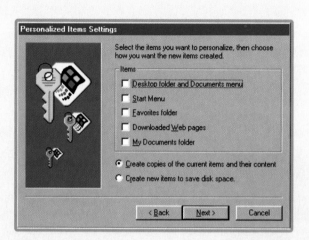

You can then select the items you want personalised for each user of the computer. If you do not select any, Windows will use the same desktop and menus for each user, but will retain personal things like passwords and Internet settings. If you select all the boxes, each user will be able to change the appearance of Windows without affecting anyone else's settings.

When you click on **'Finish'**, the computer will restart and you will be presented with a login box (below). Simply type in the username and password you keyed in earlier and you can now log in as a new user. You can then customise Windows to your own preferences.

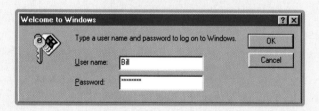

Security issues

Unfortunately, even with the multi-users' set-up, the log-in and password for each user does not protect any of the PC's files from unauthorised access. By using DOS or the Windows Explorer software you can still look at any file, irrespective of what log-in and password you supply. To protect files, you need to purchase additional encryption software or shareware and then protect groups of files or folders with a password.

ACTIVE DESKTOP

Windows 98 now has a feature that can integrate web content into the PC desktop. Entitled Active Desktop, it allows popular web content such as news sites and software updates to be downloaded automatically from the World Wide Web. Active Desktop is very powerful and can be customised to change how Windows interacts with the Web and the user interface.

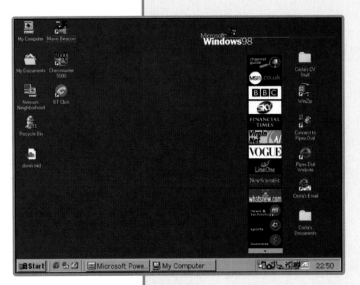

This is a typical Active Desktop-enabled screen. The bar on the right of the screen is a list of channels you can access quickly by simply clicking on each. You can add to this channel list or even add active content, which will be displayed on your desktop permanently. This content could be stock prices, weather reports or even an online magazine. To add an active channel you need to follow these steps.

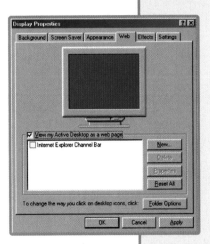

Adding an Active Desktop channel

1. Right-click on the desktop, select **'Properties'**, then select **'Web'** from the tabs along the top.

2. From this new window, select the **'New'** button. A confirmation will appear, asking whether you want to go to Microsoft's online gallery of Active Desktop components. Selecting **'Yes'** should initiate an Internet connection and open the gallery. If this fails, go online manually and start again from step 1.

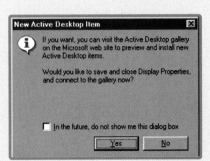

3. The Active Desktop Gallery has several categories of content including news, sports, weather and travel. You can browse the available content by clicking on a category and the options within it. Once you have decided upon your selection, select **'Add to Active desktop'** to add what you need to your desktop.

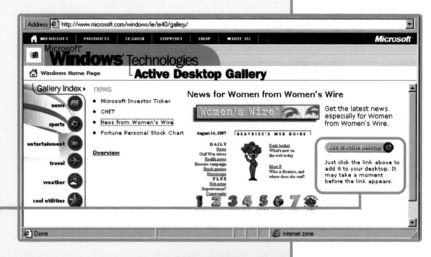

4. The selected Active Desktop material can now be added to your desktop. You will be asked for a confirmation and will have the opportunity to customise its operation, using the **'Customise Subscription'** button. From here you can specify when a subscription should be updated automatically and what type of content you would like displayed.

The update process requires the PC to go online and pull new information off the Internet. When the upload is complete, your new channel will be added to your desktop.

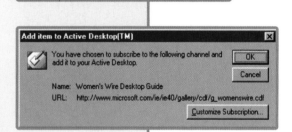

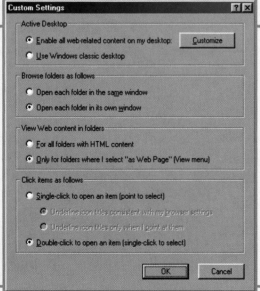

Changing your Active Desktop settings

Active Desktop allows many more options for customising the way Windows behaves.

To access these settings, right-click on the desktop and select **'Custom Settings'**.

This allows you to see extra information about folders and documents, including the ability to preview images as you highlight their icons.

You can also get the Windows interface to behave more like a web page by enabling the **'Single-click'** feature, which lets you launch applications and open documents with a single click instead of a double click, just as if you were single-clicking on a web link.

SCHEDULING ACTIVITIES

What to schedule and when

You can set up many different types of tasks for the scheduler to perform. The wizard in the 'Schedule Task' utility lists the options you can choose from depending on the software installed on your machine. Common tasks include disk scan, defragmentation and full anti-virus sweep, and they should be performed about once a month.

Some computer housekeeping activities such as scanning disks for errors or viruses are often overlooked. With the scheduling software provided with Windows, these boring jobs can be automatically carried out when the PC is not in use. This section explains how to set the scheduler up to do this.

How to schedule activities

In order to schedule activities you need to run the **'Schedule Task'** utility (to find it, click first on **'Start'**, then **'Programs'**, **'Accessories'** and **'System Tools'**). Simply double-clicking on the **'Add Scheduled Task'** icon allows you to set up particular programs or events to occur at scheduled times or during times of inactivity.

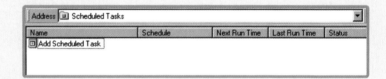

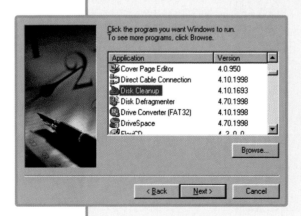

A useful wizard guides you through the various options available. Simply respond to the prompts requested by the wizard to set up a scheduled task.

Windows then works out which programs can be automatically run by the scheduler and comes up with a list of applications that came with the Windows installation CD-ROM; you can add others by selecting **'Browse'**, then picking a program. Additional software that you have installed can be found under C:\Windows\Start Menu\Programs.

3 | Customising your PC

70

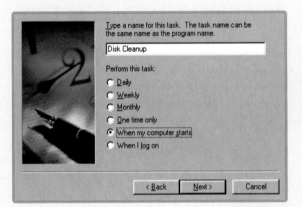

Once you choose the program to add to the task scheduler (in the example below **'Disk Cleanup'**), you are asked to give a name to the task and specify how often you would like it to be run.

When schedules clash

The schedule utility is a useful time-saver. However, if your scheduled task starts while you are running another application you may generate an unexpected error, causing your machine to crash. For example, running a scheduled task such as a virus update may well interrupt the download of a file from the Internet. You can toggle the scheduled tasks between active and pause simply by right-clicking on the schedule icon (in the bottom right-hand corner) and selecting the pause/un-pause option.

After the wizard guides you through the entire process of setting up a scheduled task, you are prompted by a dialog box which confirms all the options you have chosen. A new task-manager icon appears on the Taskbar.

You can check on what tasks you have planned by double-clicking on the task-manager icon at any time.

HARDWARE PROFILES

Some computer peripherals, such as personal digital assistants (PDAs) and digital cameras, are not always attached to a PC. To make adding and removing these devices simpler, Windows has a built-in configuration manager that can be assigned various profiles, e.g. you may have a games profile, which enables your joystick and 3D glasses and simultaneously disables the printer and scanner because your PC may not be able to use all the devices at the same time or you may want to save memory resources by not loading unused devices. This section explains how to set up multiple profiles.

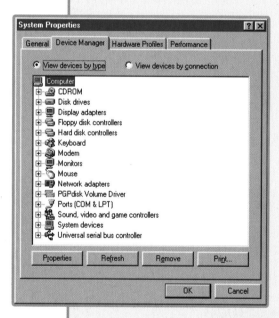

To activate a new hardware profile, first right-click on the **'My Computer'** icon and then select **'Properties'**. From here you can look at all the hardware devices you have installed on your system. Most computer systems' hardware profiles do not change a great deal. However, laptop users with docking stations, containing extra devices such as a CD-ROM, or extra hard disk, and those whose computer systems have many removable devices may benefit from setting up alternative profiles.

Click on the **'Hardware Profiles'** tab and then click on **'Copy'** to make a copy of your original profile. This is the profile with the most common hardware set-up and is the default on your PC.

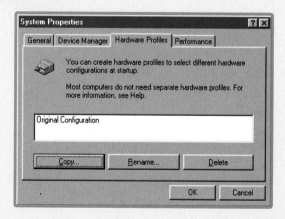

3 | Customising your PC

Now give this new configuration a unique name. In the example on the left, some computerised music equipment which requires some tweaking of settings to get it to work properly is being set up, so over **'Original Configuration'** the name **'music equipment'** is typed in.

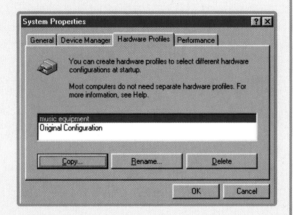

The new configuration appears in the box on the left. You now need to shut down and restart your system in the normal way to access your new profile.

When Windows restarts, before the loading screen appears you are prompted to specify which configuration you would like to use.

Windows cannot determine the hardware configuration of this computer.
Please choose one of the following:
1. Orginal configuration
2. Music equipment
3. None of the above

Enter your selection

In the example, by selecting option 2 (**'Music equipment'**) when Windows loads, you can add new devices or a docking station without altering your original 'safe' configuration. If you make any mistakes, providing you remove any additional hardware, restarting the system and selecting **'Original configuration'** will take you back to the profile as it was before you tinkered with it.

DISK CACHING

Disk caching is a method of improving the speed at which data moves from the hard disk into your computer's RAM memory. Caching works by storing commonly used files in memory, so the data can be accessed faster. Although this is done automatically, customising the caching feature will maximise performance.

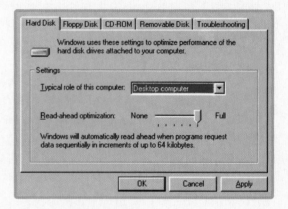

To access the caching option, right-click on **'My Computer'** and select **'Properties'**, **'Performance'** and then **'File System'**. At this new menu, you can change the amount of **'Read-ahead optimization'** (cache). The more cache used, the faster the performance of the system. Conversely, if your machine has only a small amount of RAM (less then 32Mb), you should reduce this cache to help complex programs work properly.

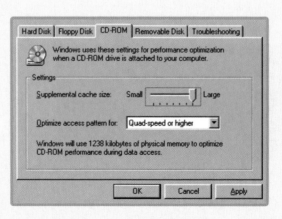

The same caching principle can be applied to the CD-ROM drive to improve its performance.

Warning!

If you are using caching software that you have bought, you have to disable the Windows built-in caching utility for the new software to work correctly.

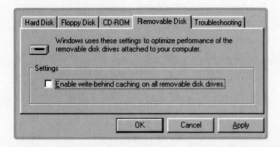

Caching can also be applied to removable devices, such as zip drives and floppy disks. If you do not have any of these devices or if you use them only rarely, you can disable this type of caching by unclicking the box that enables caching (see above).

Although this is not strictly part of disk caching, you can improve the speed of the Windows start-up by disabling the automatic search for removable drives when the system first starts.

POWER MANAGEMENT

Modern PCs are designed to be left on permanently. However, like a video recorder, when a PC is not in use it can automatically go into a sleep mode that draws less electricity. This section explains the fundamentals of power management and how to configure your system for standby mode.

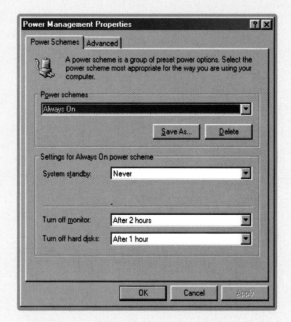

Using Power Management tools

Controlling the electricity consumption of your PC is essential from an environmental point of view. To do so, select the '**Power Management**' icon that can be found in the Control Panel under '**Settings**' from the '**Start**' menu. You can then customise various key settings on your computer which cater to your individual needs and usage (e.g. if you have to leave your PC on to receive faxes but are not using the system, you can set up Power Management schemes that will save electricity consumption).

Modern monitors tend to use a lot of electricity. You can manually set the period of inactivity which automatically turns your monitor to a low-power 'standby' mode.

Advanced Power Management

If you click on the **'Advanced'** tab you can choose to have a power meter displayed on the Taskbar. This is useful for laptop users to help gauge how much power is left in the battery pack. You can also set up an option to have the computer ask for a password when you want to get into the system after it has been in standby mode — this is to prevent other people from using your machine without permission.

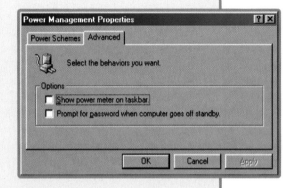

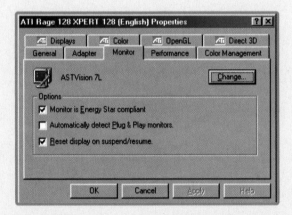

Individual graphics cards have their own customisable power-management options, which can be found by right-clicking the desktop and selecting **'Properties'**. The graphics card can send power-management commands to monitors to turn them off, if they support this function. Some older monitors may fail to start properly after being in low-power mode; to correct this problem make sure the **'Reset display'** option is ticked.

WINDOWS SCHEMES

With the help of 'Windows Schemes', a feature which enables you to make your PC as individual as you, you can vary graphics, sounds and icons used by Windows to display items.

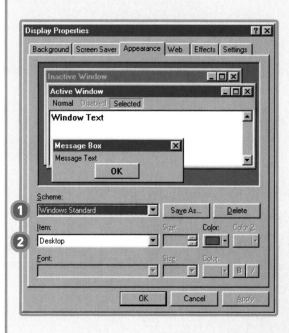

Selecting and using Windows Schemes

In order to select and use Windows Schemes, right-click on the Windows desktop and select **'Properties'**. In the **'Display Properties'** dialog box select the **'Appearance'** tab and you are presented with the following options:

1 If you click on the **'Scheme'** drop-down dialog box, you are presented with a list of ready-made options for colours and font sizes. These schemes have names such as 'rose' and 'storm'. If you click on, say, rose, the colour of the dialog boxes will turn from the Windows standard blue to a pink.

2 If you click on the **'Item'** drop-down box, you are presented with more options (see left) to customise individual items. You can e.g. change the size and colour scheme of a message box or the Scroll Bar.

Changing and exploring sounds

Many events and occurrences in
Windows are accompanied by
sounds. You can, if you wish, vary the
default settings either to turn off the
sounds or to change them.

To test or change the sounds used by your PC,
select the **'Sound'** icon in the Control Panel (click
on **'Start'** and then **'Settings'**). You can preview
various sounds by using the play and stop buttons.
You can assign different sounds to different events
and save this information as your own personal
scheme. Simply select an event which defines a
particular action being carried out (e.g. exiting
Windows) and then assign a sound you would like
to hear when that event occurs.

ACCESSIBILITY OPTIONS

The 'Accessibility Options' feature in Windows provides help for users who have sight or hearing impairments or limited dexterity. They can choose to have, say, large fonts, visual cues replacing audio cues, or adapted keyboards. This section looks at how to configure Accessibility Options.

To change Accessibility Options, click on **'Start'**, then **'Settings'**, **'Control Panel'** and then the **'Accessibility Options'** icon.

The keyboard options are useful for people who have limited dexterity.

The **'StickyKeys'** feature removes the need to hold down special keys such as Ctrl or Alt while typing another character. Usually, to copy data you hold Ctrl and press C; with **'StickyKeys'** you press Ctrl first, then C separately, to achieve the same thing.

If you have difficulty typing and tend to hold keys down longer than necessary, you can make Windows ignore the extra keystrokes by using the **'FilterKeys'** option.

More information

For more information on Accessibility Options in Windows, click on the 'Start' menu and select 'Help'. At the prompt, type in 'Accessibility', and then double-click on any entries you want to explore further.

The **'Sound'** options replace audio cues with visual ones and *vice versa*. These options work in some applications.

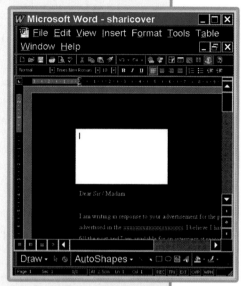

With the **'High Contrast'** mode activated,
Windows looks like the example on the right.
This mode is helpful for partially sighted
users.

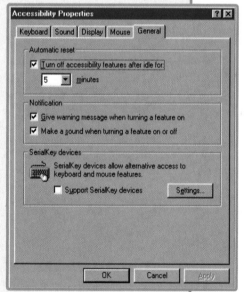

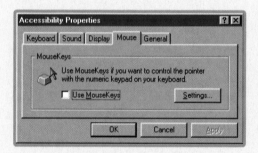

The **'Mouse'** option allows you to use
the keyboard or numeric keypad
instead of the mouse.

The **'General'** tab covers other
useful Accessibility Options such
as audio warnings when features
are turned on and off.

MAKING YOUR PC KID-SAFE

The PC can be a great way for children to learn and to communicate with others, via the Internet. But there are certain parts of the Internet where they could be exposed to pornography, foul language or the activities of undesirables. The PC is quite resilient to children altering its settings, but some areas of Windows are much better left undisturbed. This section looks at how you can help your kids have a good time using your PC while minimising the risks.

Warning!

Children should not be left unsupervised with an Internet connection. Computers are inherently flexible and most of the restrictions you impose on your offspring's Internet usage can be circumvented. Often, education is the best form of protection.

Protecting important files from tiny fingers

The first step to take is to make access to the computer by password. The simplest way to restrict access to your PC is with a BIOS password (see section 5.2). With this password activated, if the PC is turned on, it will not start until the password has been entered.

When your children want to use the computer, it is wise to give them their own login name and user area (for more detail see section 3.3). When you create a user area, all your applications and settings are duplicated. However, if you log in as another user you can remove directories containing important documents and delete items from the start menu to prevent access.

In case your children accidentally delete them, it is wise to create a new partition on the drive in which to keep important or sensitive files. You can do this with an encryption application such as PGP. With this software you can create virtual hard drives on your main drive which can be opened only with a password.

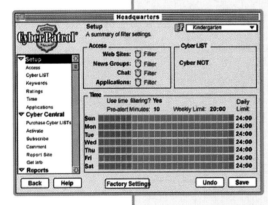

Screening out Internet dangers

Many of the Internet service providers now offer parental control and restrictions on Internet browsing, designed to give parents more peace of mind when their kids are unsupervised on the Internet. For a monthly fee, companies such as AOL will allow you to restrict your child's browsing to sites it deems safe. Access is controlled by passwords.

A cheaper option is to buy a program such as Netnanny or CyberPatrol. These programs act as a barrier between your Internet connection and sites not suitable for young people. With these packages you can set the types of content you want to screen out and the software will block sites that contain this type of information. However, the software is not 100 per cent effective and fees are charged for updates.

Removing clutter from the desktop

You can download from the Internet a useful piece of free software called TweakGUI. This application allows you to customise the desktop of any user. With TweakGUI you can remove applications that you don't want your kids to access from their desktop.

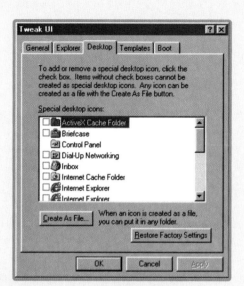

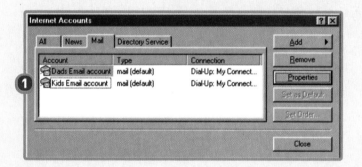

Physical protection for your PC

To stop children opening up your PC you can fit security screws that require a specially shaped key to undo them.

You can also buy a special lock for the floppy drive and remove the CD-ROM drive from the BIOS to prevent children from installing software without your knowledge.

Screening email

When you have created settings for your children to use, make sure that you remove any personal information from email signatures. Details such as user name and address should be excluded from email used by children.

You can also set up your email so that you can access your child's email account from your email account.

1 Create a new connection in your email program using your children's email details.

2 Change both your own and your children's advanced settings so that email messages are not removed from your ISP's server for at least 7 days.

Now when you log on all your email and your children's email will be downloaded into your email inbox.

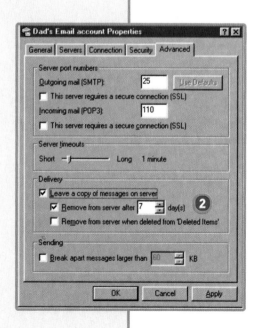

Many complex tasks go on inside a modern PC. As the flexibility increases, so does the possibility for errors and unforeseen problems. Anomalies or bugs — such as the Y2K one, which caused computers to malfunction because of the date change (to '00') at the end of the 20th century — can affect almost all software applications and operating systems under certain conditions. The first thing to do if your PC seems to be performing oddly is to determine whether it is because of a bug or just an unusual feature — or, indeed, an oversight on your part while you were trying to perform a task.

Every software application, and Windows itself, has an accompanying manual or help file holding a good deal of information, but if this fails to help you can use a simple diagnostic software tool to find the problem.

Some problems are very common and can be fixed even with very limited technical knowledge. In this section we look at the basics of troubleshooting and explain how to find the information that will enable you to reach a diagnosis.

BASIC TROUBLESHOOTING

4.1 Fault or quirk of Windows?
Sometimes Windows behaves oddly. Deciding whether this is a
fault or just an unusual feature is the first step in troubleshooting.

4.2 Testing your PC
This section explains how the various ports on your PC
work and how to fix common connection problems.

4.3 Diagnostic tools
How Windows' built-in software can help diagnose a problem.

4.4 Terminating an errant program
Sometimes programs crash: this section explains how
to end a program that is causing errors.

4.5 Fixing application errors
How to overcome common software problems.

4.6 Fixing printer problems
What to check and how to fix common printer problems.

4.7 Fixing scanner problems
Solutions to common scanner problems.

4.8 Fixing graphics problems
How to approach graphics problems.

4.9 Fixing sound problems
From no sound to poor-quality sound, this section
could have the answer.

4.10 Updating Windows
How to update Windows, automatically.

4.11 Troubleshooting Word
Tips for Microsoft's popular word-processing package.

4.12 Troubleshooting for games-players (I)
Tips for fixing common games problems.

4.13 Troubleshooting for games-players (II)
More advanced tips for fixing games problems.

FAULT OR QUIRK OF WINDOWS?

Sometimes Windows may appear to be behaving oddly, but is often just performing a housekeeping task or demonstrating a feature. Before re-installing software, or opening up the case and ripping out hardware, you need to determine whether the problem is actually a fault or just a quirk of Windows. To diagnose faults you need to know about common Windows operations which can otherwise appear to be errors.

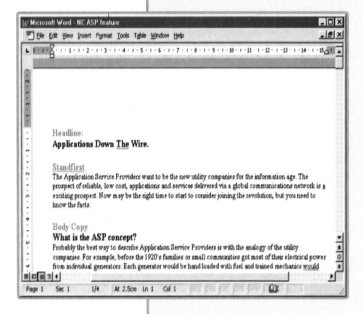

Basic troubleshooting

Missing toolbar

In the example to the left toolbars have been turned off. This can occur if you select the wrong menu option or press the wrong key combination. The toolbars can easily be restored if you look at the View menu and select Toolbars. Just select the ones you want to see (the defaults are to show Standard and Formatting).

Character overwriting when typing

Usually if the cursor is placed within the middle of a sentence and you start typing, the remainder of the sentence gets pushed along by the text you type. If you see each character you type replacing the existing text, character by character, you have pressed the Insert key by accident. This key changes the text mode from the usual one of Insert to a mode called Overtype. Press the Insert key again to return things to normal.

Number pad not working

Are strange things happening when you try to type in numbers from the keypad? Does the cursor jump around the page at random? Are characters being deleted? Check the lights on the keyboard, particularly the NumLock light and Scroll Lock. The chances are that these have been turned on/off and the keys have taken on an entirely different function.

Files start oddly

Sometimes double-clicking on a document just does not do what you expect. It may activate a different application, or Windows may ask you for the name of the application with which it should open the file. The cause may be a change in the program/document relationship. When you double-click a document saved, say, in Word, Windows makes sure that Word is the program it uses to re-open the document. Most applications use a file-name suffix to indicate this, e.g. .DOC for Microsoft Word, .XLS for Microsoft Excel or .BMP (bitmap) for graphics programs. A newly installed application may try to take over the association with a particular file format. Within the preferences of any new software you may see options for file associations under the guise of extensions, usually under an Options menu choice or sometimes under Preferences. File associations can be altered manually via the Folder Options menu on any Windows Explorer window (click on the File Types tab). See section 2.3 and File Types at back of book.

Turning on features

Quite often, odd behaviour in Windows or one of its many applications results from an obscure feature being turned on accidentally. Sometimes, the application's Help file can provide the answer (see example opposite, from within Word, with the disappearing toolbars). In the Toolbar's Help menu, under Contents, you can type 'displaying' or 'hiding', which are in the list of topics: this can be a good place to start if you encounter this kind of problem.

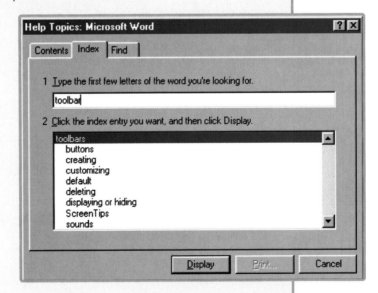

Help Topics: Microsoft Word

Contents | Index | Find

1 Type the first few letters of the word you're looking for.

`toolbar`

2 Click the index entry you want, and then click Display.

toolbars
  buttons
  creating
  customizing
  default
  deleting
  displaying or hiding
  ScreenTips
  sounds

Display | Print... | Cancel

TESTING YOUR PC

Power on testing

The most likely time for a PC to break down is while it is starting up (booting). The computer runs a series of tests on each piece of hardware before loading the operating system. If a device fails the Power-On-Self-Test (POST), it may cause the machine to stop the booting procedure. The POST normally shows messages that say which devices have passed testing and which have failed.

Warning!

To save energy, some computers turn themselves off if left unattended. Pressing the keyboard or mouse starts the computer up again.

Common causes of PC problems are loose or faulty connections between external devices and the main system unit. Good troubleshooting practice is to check all the connections and peripherals before moving on to more advanced troubleshooting.

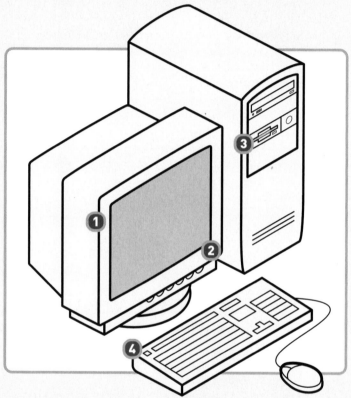

Computer fails to start when 'on' button is pressed

1 Check the screen Read any information displayed on the screen. Some systems may require a password or particular key to be depressed before you are allowed to continue.

2 Is the monitor on? Your computer system unit may be working but your monitor may either be off or have suffered a failure. Monitors tend to last 3—5 years.

3 Remove floppy disk If you use a 3¹/₂-inch floppy disk to transfer work, remove it before turning off or starting up your PC.

4 Examine keyboard If a key has been stuck in the 'down' position this can prevent a computer from starting correctly.

5 Check mains power Ensure that the mains is switched on. Use a bedside lamp or clock to test that the plug socket still has power.

6 **Monitor connection** A 15-pin cable connects your monitor to the system unit. Ensure that the cable is connected. The plug will only go in one way so do not force anything that seems tight.

7 **Power to system unit** A three-wire power cable normally runs from the mains to the system unit. Many PCs also have a power cable that runs from the system unit to the monitor (screen). Ensure that this is not loose.

8 **Peripheral connection** The back of your PC has connections for a mouse and a keyboard. These connectors are very similar in design — round in shape, with 6 holes. They should be marked for easy identification. If not, finding the right one through trial and error will not damage your PC. The mouse may instead work by a wider 9-pin connector called the serial port. This connection is sometimes used for modems.

9 **Device connection** A longer 25-hole connector, called a parallel port, is standard on desktop PCs. This is commonly used for printers and scanners.

Bits and PCs

A PC computer system consists of only 9 major components. The chance of more than one component failing simultaneously is minuscule.

Protecting the PSU

The PSU (Power Supply Unit) is essentially a transformer, converting mains voltage to the 5, 9 or 12 volts used by your system unit. Irregular mains supply and rare occurrences like lightning or blackouts can damage the PSU and connected computer equipment. A UPS (Uninterruptible Power Supply) or surge protector can help protect vulnerable systems.

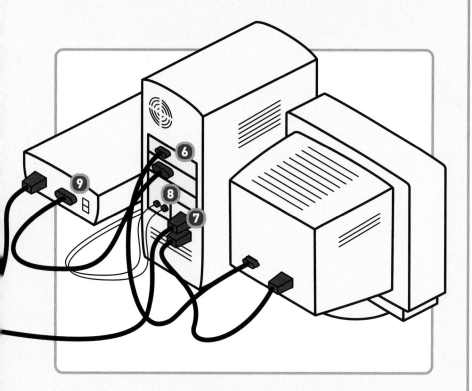

DIAGNOSTIC TOOLS

When Windows does have a problem, finding the cause of the error can be time-consuming. The operating system contains several software tools that can help with problems within software applications and hardware devices. This section explains how to access these tools and understand the information provided by them.

The Microsoft System Information tool comes free with some versions of Windows 98 and with several Microsoft applications. The utility can be found in the c:\program files\common files\Microsoft shared\msinfo folder under the name Msinfo32.exe. Many of the options and features are very technical; however, the accompanying help file is very useful.

The msinfo program gives you a detailed description of each application, whether it is running in memory or on the hard disk: the description includes its name, version number, who created the program and what it does. Sometimes an application generates an error message. With msinfo you can find out what the application does and which company created the application so you can contact it for technical support. By having the version number of an application you can look on the manufacturer's web site for a newer version of the application if the version you have is producing errors.

1 The Windows Report tool creates a complete analysis of your Windows system (what is running, your default printer, and so on).

2 If you have applied a Windows update which is not working properly, this option removes the update.

3 This tool checks important Windows files for possible corruption.

4 The signature verification tool is used mostly by developers, seldom for troubleshooting.

5 The registry contains thousands of individual program settings: this utility checks for errors.

6 This option, for Windows experts only, is used to make the system ignore device drivers at start-up.

7 Dr Watson is a useful utility for monitoring the system and detecting

1 Windows Report Tool
2 Update Wizard Uninstall
3 System File Checker
4 Signature Verification Tool
5 Registry Checker
6 Automatic Skip Driver Agent
7 Dr. Watson
8 System Configuration Utility
9 ScanDisk
10 Version Conflict Manager

errors. It uses a small amount of processor and memory capacity.

8 The system configuration utility changes the way in which Windows starts up and shuts down. It is inadvisable to alter these settings.

9 See section 2.2.

10 When you install new system drivers, the old versions are often backed up by the system. This utility can restore these older versions if necessary.

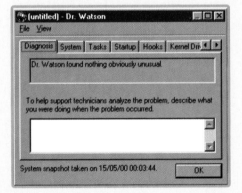

Dr Watson

The Dr Watson utility automatically scans your system for errors. When running it leaves a small icon in the bottom right-hand corner of the task bar. If a program crashes, clicking on this icon may help you find out why the error has occurred.

TERMINATING AN ERRANT PROGRAM

The complexity and flexibility of modern software applications running in Windows means that occasionally the software will crash (i.e. an error has occurred). When a program crashes, you may need to shut it down manually to continue using Windows. The termination of the application is normally automatic. However, if the application crash is more serious, you will need to take steps to recover it, as described in this section.

Sometimes a program stops working and closes down; sometimes, when a program stops working, it prevents the system from functioning properly. You can manually shut down applications via the **'Close Program'** feature. To try to close down an application, follow these steps.

Step 1 Hold down the Ctrl + Alt keys then tap the Delete key just once. After a few seconds the **'Close Program'** box should appear. If a program has crashed badly, the **'Close Program'** box may not appear. If a program has crashed and the **'Close Program'** box has not appeared, all you can do is turn off the power from the system and then restart. If an application or Windows task continually crashes, you may need to re-install it.

Step 2 If the **'Close Program'** box does appear, look for applications with 'Not responding' next to them. To shut these applications down, select the non-responding program and then click on **'End Task'**. Again, after a short wait, the applications should shut down and return control back to the user. You can check this by using the Ctrl + Alt + Delete keys to bring back up the **'Close Program'** box and check whether the application has closed successfully. Before continuing to use the PC, restart it in the normal way.

Step 3 If the application will not end, follow Step 1 but choose the **'Shut Down'** option instead of **'End Task'**. This option shuts down all applications, and attempts to shut down your PC, after which you can restart the PC. This is sometimes necessary because certain tasks cannot terminate while other tasks are still running.

Why do programs crash?

Although modern software is far more reliable than that run on the punchcard-driven computers of the 1970s, most applications will still crash under certain circumstances. The reason may be bad programming within the millions of lines of computer code which make up each program. Sometimes an error occurs when applications try to communicate with each other, possibly because of differences in the versions of the programs: such so-called 'conflicts' are common. However, the most frequent cause of crashes is user interaction. Most software companies actively encourage users to report problems that occur when users find new ways to interact with software, so that the problems can be fixed for subsequent versions.

FIXING APPLICATION ERRORS

Some software applications/programs crash constantly under certain circumstances. All software has relationships with parts of the Windows operating system, hardware devices and other software. Often, to solve an application error, you need to fix the underlying cause of the error. To do this you have to understand the relationships between the applications and how to test each part of Windows to see if it is working correctly.

COMMON PROBLEMS AND POSSIBLE CAUSES

Programs crash unexpectedly

• Try closing any other applications which may be running in the background or on the Taskbar, then try running the application again.

• Try restarting Windows, followed by running a full ScanDisk to correct any problems on the hard disk. See section 2.2.

• Remove applications from the Startup group (see section 2.10) and restart Windows, then restart the system before testing the errant application again.

• Check the application's manual or help files for a **'known errors'** or **'troubleshooting'** section.

Program won't start

• Some applications require the original installation CD-ROM to be present in the drive before the application will start (this is an anti-piracy measure).

• Some applications depend on a hardware device being live before they can function correctly. For example, scanning software may need the scanner to be activated

before the program can start.

• Some applications require the screen resolution and colour depth to be set to the correct values before the software starts (see section 3.2).

• Some older programs work only in DOS. Try creating a DOS session and running the application again. See section 5.8.

Application file won't save

- If you try to save a file which is used by another application, Windows may prevent this from happening.
- Some types of files, especially graphics formats, can take up tens of megabytes of space. For example, trying to save an image from a scanner on to a floppy disk is not possible if the image is greater than 1.44Mb in size.
- Files can be locked into a read-only mode by users or other applications. Trying to save a new file with the same name as the locked file may cause an error. Try saving the file with a new name or to a different location on the hard drive.

Application display looks garbled

- Some applications may appear garbled or unreadable. For better results, try changing the screen resolution, as outlined in section 3.2.
- Older DOS applications often look odd when displayed in a window. Try maximising the window displaying the application or restarting the system in DOS mode. See section 5.8 for more information on DOS.
- Each application may support many different viewing options. Look for a menu option called **'View'** or under **'Options'** or **'Preferences'**.

Troubleshooting tips

- Check for viruses
- Use the software help files
- Look for the **'readme'** file for **'known errors'**
- Restart Windows
- Re-install the application
- Contact technical support for the application
- Examine the web site of the errant application for technical assistance or a newer version of the software.

Why a menu feature does not work

- Some features such as cut/copy need a piece of text, or other item selected on the screen before they become highlighted.

- If you have a lower-price or demo version of a software package certain advanced features may be disabled, despite appearing on the menu (check the menu's help or version options: telltale words include 'limited edition', 'demo' or 'beta version').

- If you load a file which has been set by another user for viewing only into an application, some of the editing/saving options may have been restricted, to prohibit changes.

- You may need to add additional parts, known as plug-ins, for some features of applications: these are sometimes provided free of charge.

FIXING PRINTER PROBLEMS

Modern printers are generally reliable but breakdowns do occur. The printer relies on both internal electronics and software drivers residing within Windows to function correctly. To fix a printer problem, you will probably need to look at both hardware and software settings. This section looks at the commonest printer problems and how to solve them.

COMMON PROBLEMS AND POSSIBLE CAUSES

Is the printer plugged into the correct socket?
Most modern printers use either the parallel or the USB socket for connection to the PC. Make sure the cable is securely fitted between PC and printer.

Is the paper correctly loaded?
Are the sheets sticking together?
Many basic printers accept up to 100 sheets of paper within the paper feed. You may sometimes need to riffle one corner of a new batch of paper to loosen the sheets before reloading the paper tray.

Has the right paper type been selected within the application?
Printers can accept many sizes of paper. Within the printer options within an application, make sure that the paper size matches the paper loaded into the printer.

Is the print quality poor?
• Check the ink level of the printer cartridges.
• Many printers have a self-cleaning mode (check the manual for how to start this mode: normally, you need to hold down a button for three seconds).
• Look in the driver options for different 'quality' modes, such as draft, standard and high quality, and select the one you want.
• With ink printers, if one colour fails the printed image may start to look odd, with some colours missing entirely. You may need to replace an ink cartridge.

Is the printer switched on and 'online'?
The printer must be switched on and also turned to 'online'. 'Online' means that it is able to receive data. When a printer is online a small light or other visual indication normally appears.

Is the printer driver installed and set as the default printer?
Each printer has an associated piece of driving software. Make sure your printer driver is installed and set as the default. Follow the guide on the opposite page.

Has the right paper source been selected?
Most printers have a second paper feed for single sheets, such as letterheads. Select which feed (or tray) to use within the printing section of the application.

Setting the default printer

Click on the start menu, select Control Panel, then select Printers. From here, right-click on the printer icon which matches your make and model of printer and select **'Set as Default'**. If this icon is not here, consult the manual that came with your printer.

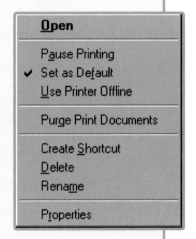

Typical print options

These options are normally accessible from the File menu under Print.

1 Paper size

2 Paper source

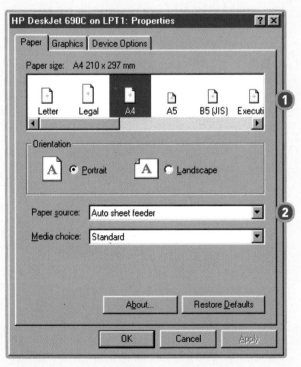

FIXING SCANNER PROBLEMS

The optical scanner takes paper-based images and converts them into digital images. A scanner can connect to a PC in various ways, and there are several methods of controlling the internal electronics for scanning and transferring data to the PC. Even though scanners vary between manufacturers, taking some simple troubleshooting steps can solve many of the common problems.

COMMON PROBLEMS AND POSSIBLE CAUSES

Is the scanner plugged into the computer?
Check all the connections between the PC and the scanner.

If the scanner is connected via the printer, are both devices switched on?
Many older scanners use the printer port for scanning. You need to ensure that both devices are switched on before turning on your PC.

Is the application scanning the document using the correct settings?
Most scanner problems are related to the software controlling the scanner. Common problems include having the resolution (DPI) setting too high, causing massive files, 100s of megabytes in size, to be created.

Has the scanner been unlocked since transportation?
Scanners have a locking feature for transportation. Check the scanner manual on how to lock and unlock your scanner during and after transportation.

Is there enough space on the hard disk for the image to be saved?
Scanners can produce very large image files. If you have insufficient hard disk or memory space to accommodate these files an error may be generated. Try reducing the number of colours and the resolution (DPI) of the scanner.

Each driver will vary depending on manufacturer but most of the features are common

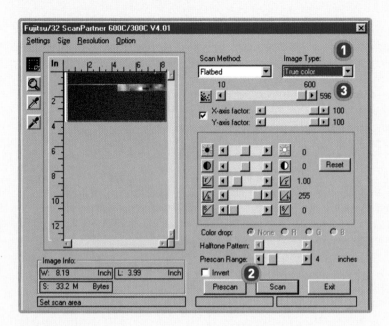

Is another application affecting the scanner software?

Scanners that use the parallel port can sometimes conflict with the software that controls the printer. The printer software is often represented as a small icon along the Taskbar (bottom right). Try disabling this software first, then trying the scanner again.

1 'Image Type' allows you to set the number of colours to include in the scan. The higher the colour depth, the bigger the file. Hence, 'True color' creates a scan with over 16 million shades of colour. This is useful if you are scanning and reproducing a photographic image using a photographic printer. However, when scanning low-quality material or for output to the screen, lower colour depth produces much more manageable file sizes.

2 Many scanner drivers present a preview of the image to be scanned. You can normally fine-tune this by selecting an area within the preview scan and then selecting either 'Prescan' or 'Scan'.

3 The DPI (dots per inch) also affects the quality of the scan and the size of the file. As a rule of thumb, if you are scanning for on-screen uses such as creating images for a web site, the DPI needs to be only around 75 because of the limitations of a computer monitor. If, however, you are scanning for a printed version, you should use a higher DPI, and one that is divisible by your printer's print resolution — e.g. if you have a 600 DPI printer, scanning at either 300 or 600 DPI will give you results as good as scanning at much higher resolutions but without creating very big files.

FIXING GRAPHICS PROBLEMS

The graphics system of a modern PC is essential for multimedia-rich applications such as games and computer-aided design. Graphics standards are evolving at a rapid pace. Some of the most common standards include Microsoft's DirectX and the Open GL standard. Each application has hardware requirements added to these graphics standards that must be met for the software to work correctly. This section covers the testing of graphics cards and fixing common problems.

COMMON PROBLEMS AND POSSIBLE CAUSES

Is the monitor plugged into the computer's VGA socket?
Check all the connections between the PC and the monitor.

Is the monitor switched on?
Check.

Is the colour depth suitable to the target application?
Many applications (especially video games) require a minimum number of colours to be displayed on the screen. If this colour depth is too low the application may look odd or not work. To get to the screen properties, right-click on the Windows desktop and select properties.

Is the hardware acceleration affecting the graphics card performance?
The display properties screen also has advanced functions. From within these advanced functions you may be able to reduce the amount of hardware acceleration offered by a graphics card. This hardware acceleration can affect the reliability of the video device within older applications.

Are the correct DirectX drivers installed?
DirectX is a standard created by Microsoft to help multimedia applications to work correctly. The DirectX software is updated by individual graphics card manufacturers to improve both performance and compatibility between software and their products. To test and update your DirectX and graphics card drivers follow the steps on the opposite page.

Is the resolution of the monitor capable of supporting the selected graphics mode?
Many multimedia applications require a minimum screen resolution. This resolution is described as a horizontal and vertical value. Check the software's requirements and compare them to the settings in your display properties.

DirectX diagnostic tools

The DirectX diagnostic tool can normally be found in the C:\Windows\systems directory. If it is not in this directory you may have to do a search using the Windows file-finder described in section 2.9. Within this utility is a section called **'DirectX Files'** which diagnoses the probable reliability of your DirectX drivers. For more information on DirectX see section 4.12. If you find a large number of warning symbols by these files (as in the example below) you may need to update your DirectX drivers to solve major problems.

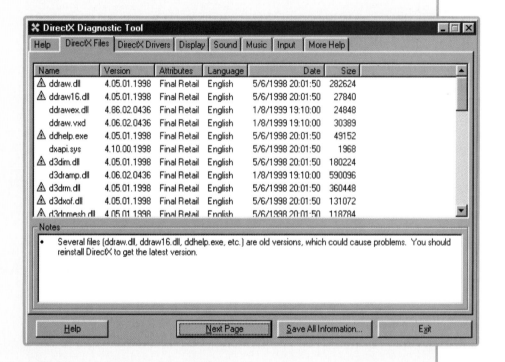

Re-installing graphics and DirectX software

STEP 1
Ascertain the make and model of your graphics card, as shown in the system information utility, which can be accessed by right-clicking on the My Computer icon or by selecting the **'system'** icon from within the control panel.

STEP 2
Ascertain which version of DirectX you are currently running. The DirectX diagnostic tool, pictured above, can help with this.

STEP 3
Look at the web site of your graphics card manufacturer for the latest graphics card driver software.

STEP 4
Look on the Microsoft web site for the latest DirectX software (it is also frequently available on CDs given away with computer magazines). To install, you may need to specify what graphics card you have.

FIXING SOUND PROBLEMS

A modern PC can play audio at up to CD quality. Soundcards are very reliable and often perform without problems for the lifetime of the PC. Problems may occur when using the soundcard for, say, creating music or recording from an analogue source (tape, CD or voice). Understanding how Windows controls the soundcard is the key to fixing the majority of audio-related problems. This section explains how soundcards work and offers practical tips for solving problems.

COMMON PROBLEMS AND POSSIBLE CAUSES

Are the speakers plugged into the correct speaker socket?
Check all the connections between the PC and the speakers.

Are the speakers switched on?
Unlike hi-fi speakers, most computer versions have separate on/off buttons.

Is the hardware working correctly with the system properties?
See sections 1.10 and 5.7 for instructions on how to examine system devices. See also **System properties** on opposite page.

Is the volume muted in the sound control?
Right-click on the small speaker icon in the bottom right-hand corner and select **'Properties'**. If the icon is not active, see section 1.8 and add the **'Volume control'** utility from the Windows Setup/ multimedia section.

Is the hardware acceleration affecting the soundcard performance?
The volume control utility may also have advanced functions. From within these advanced functions you may be able to reduce the amount of hardware acceleration offered by a soundcard. This hardware acceleration can affect the reliability of the sound device within older applications.

Have the application's own volume controls been muted?
Many applications have their own volume controls, accessible through the menu system.

Is more than one program trying to use the soundcard?
Some software applications try to take full control of the soundcard while they are running. Even if these applications have been minimised they may interfere with the sound features of any program started subsequently.

System properties (sound)

By right-clicking on **'My Computer'** and selecting **'Properties'**, then picking the **'Device Manager'** tab, you can examine the current list of devices attached to your PC.

Sound devices

Right-clicking on any of these devices brings up further information.

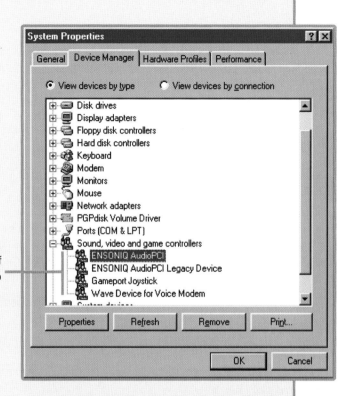

Device status

This sound device is working correctly.

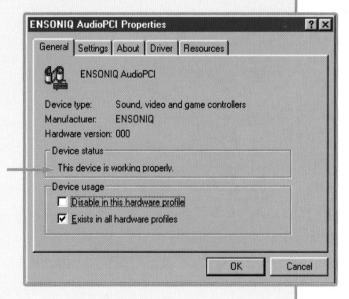

UPDATING WINDOWS

As new hardware and software devices become available, the Windows operating system may need to be updated, or upgraded, to take advantage of new features or devices. This updating process can be carried out via the web, either automatically or by manually updating the relevant parts. This section covers types of upgrades that are available and how to apply them to your Windows 98 system.

1 To access the automatic update process, all you need is an Internet connection. Click on the Start menu and then select the **'Windows Update'** option. The computer will try to connect to the Internet and go to the Microsoft Windows Update web site.

2 The Windows Update web site lists various possible upgrades and bug fixes that may be applicable to your machine. Click the tick box next to any of these files and then select **'Download'**.

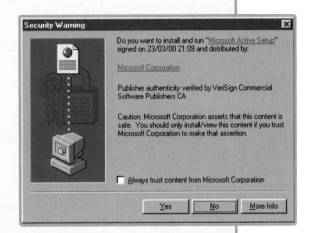

3 The web site now sends you a small program to help set up your new updates. You need to click on **'Yes'** for the update to proceed.

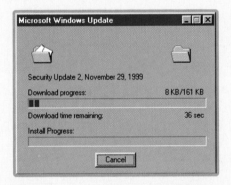

4 After the Active Setup software is downloaded, the Windows update takes place. Some additional instructions may need to be followed before the update can be completed: these will be contained within the online help file on the site or with the text files that download with the new update.

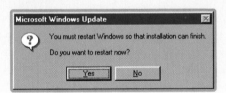

5 Restart your computer after the update procedure has finished.

Updating via disk

Although updating Windows via the Internet is the easiest way, registered Windows users can obtain an update direct from Microsoft via CD-ROM. However, these disk updates are not issued as frequently as the Internet equivalents and may incur a shipping charge.

TROUBLESHOOTING WORD

A file by any other name

Although Microsoft Word is the most commonly used word-processing program, it has many versions, to say nothing of rival programs such as WordPerfect and WordPro. This makes exchanging files between people who use different software packages cumbersome while causing formatting to become unpredictable. Moving files between PC and Apple Macintosh computers can also cause problems. To avoid problems with file incompatibility you can use various other file formats for document transfer. The most versatile is the RTF (Rich Text Format) type. This format is accepted by most word processors and is able to keep the majority of the formatting and fonts intact. To use the RTF format, simply use the 'Save as' command from your application and choose the RTF format for the document.

Microsoft Word is the most popular word-processing package in the world. Each version has offered improved features and more customisation over the previous one. But even though Word is quite a simple program, it has some quirks that can stump new users. This section answers some of the more common questions on Word.

I have spelt a word correctly, but the spell-checker insists that it is incorrect. What can I do?

The auto spell-checker in Windows often defaults to an American dictionary during installation. To change this to an English (UK) one, select from the menu bar: (Tools/Options/Spelling and Grammar), then click on the dictionaries button. You will be presented with a window where you can change the default language for the Word dictionary. Select English (UK) from the available options and then select OK.

You may have to restart Word for the changes to take effect.

My Word area is overcrowded with toolbar icons. How can I remove the ones I don't use?

Toolbars are useful for placing commonly used commands within easy reach. However, as there are over 15 different toolbars, for tasks ranging from printing to drawing graphics, you may want to display only the ones you find useful. By clicking on View/Toolbars/Customise you can add or remove toolbars and even customise what commands appear on each toolbar.

My documents look different when I print them out from how they look on screen. Why?

Print options (found under the File/Print menu, then the 'Option' button) can fix this sort of problem. The most common is **1** the 'Allow A4/Letter paper resizing' option. This option is used to reposition the text automatically if the paper in the printer does not match the page size. Turning this feature off will force Word to print to the paper without any transformation. **2** Make sure also that the 'Drawing objects' option is ticked, otherwise any graphics will not be displayed.

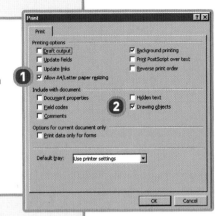

I am partially sighted and have difficulty viewing the small icons on the toolbar. Is there anything I can do about this?

By using the zoom facility you can adjust your view of the text. However, to increase the size of the icons you need to select Tools/ Customise/Options. If you tick **3** the 'Large icon' button, all toolbar icons will double in size, improving legibility.

When I opened a document I was sent, it looked odd, and when I tried to print it out half the page was missing. Why?

The computer on which the document was originally created may have had different settings. Use the View command to cycle through the possible ways to look at your document. **4** 'Page Layout' is the most commonly used mode because unlike the 'Normal' mode it will also display graphics.

It is possible that the document was designed for an A3 printer. To check this, look under File/Page Setup. **5** From this window you may need to change your page orientation to landscape while changing your paper size back to A4. This will split an A3 (portrait) document into two A4 (landscape) documents, allowing your A4 printer to output it. However, you may need to tweak margin sizes as well to get the page to fit properly.

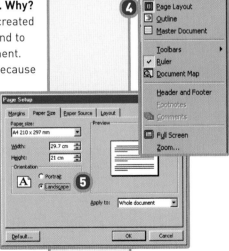

TROUBLESHOOTING FOR GAMES-PLAYERS (II)

Video games sell in comparable numbers to 'serious' software packages and today's games — from thoughtful strategy games to fast-paced 3D blast-'em-ups — appeal to people of all ages. To enhance the games-player's experience, PC hardware and software manufacturers provide additional features for improving the graphics, sound quality and speed. Underpinning much of this gaming technology is a set of standards called Microsoft DirectX. This section covers basic troubleshooting using DirectX.

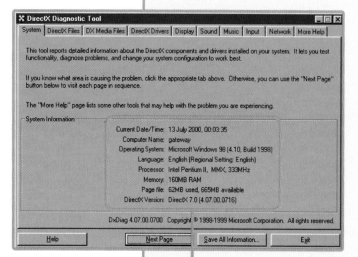

The DirectX software is normally installed along with new games. Within this software is a useful tool for running diagnostics on your system and on the various parts of DirectX. To start this diagnostic tool, click on **'Run'** from the Start button and type **DXDIAG**. If the program illustrated here fails to run, you need to run the Find File program (see section 2.9) to locate the file DXDIAG then run it from its location.

Try before you buy

Before spending perhaps as much as £40 on a computer game, check out the reviews and buying advice in magazines, which also often give away demos of games on CDs. You can also try these using downloads from the Internet.

The first page of information describes what DirectX believes your system has by way of resources. Make sure that this information matches your installed operating system, processor type and speed and available memory, and the version of DirectX installed. You also need to compare this information with the requirements of the game. If your system specification barely matches the requirements of the game, no matter how much tweaking you do the game still may not work (games developers tend to be optimistic about the minimum requirements for their games to work). If your system has enough resources, next you need to test the various parts of DirectX.

The three tabs after the system tab **(DirectX Files, DX Media Files** and **DirectX Drivers)** define the current version of DirectX you are using. You may find a great deal of variance in these version numbers. Ignore the very first digit of the version number. Most of your drivers will be greater than version 7 of DirectX. If there are any problems with your drivers (i.e. if they are corrupted) the Notes box may provide information on possible errors.

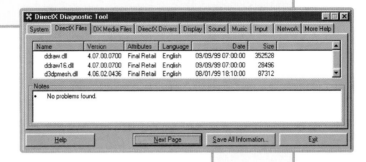

The 'Display' tab provides information on your graphics card and the games-related features.

1 The Device information box holds data about your graphics card. Compare this information with the game requirements to ensure you have sufficient resources to run it.

2 The Drivers box lists the version number of the software that controls your graphics card. Newer games may need a more recent version, which you can download from the card manufacturer's web site.

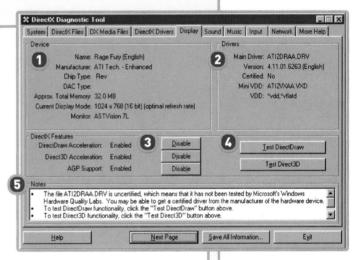

3 Action games often need hardware acceleration for improved performance, but similar acceleration can stop older games from working. Try disabling the acceleration options. The performance may be degraded but for non-action games this may not be noticeable.

4 The DXDIAG software allows you to test both the accelerated drawing and 3D functions of your graphics card. Clicking on either of these buttons will initialise various tests. If these tests fail, you may have a faulty graphics card or out-of-date drivers for your graphics card.

5 Try the Notes section, the **'readme'** file on the installation CD-ROM or the web sites of the games manufacturers.

TROUBLESHOOTING FOR GAMES-PLAYERS (II)

Know your rights

PC games manufacturers cannot test their games with every possible combination of hardware and software. If you buy a game and, despite troubleshooting, it still does not work, you can return it for a refund or credit. Even if the shop tests the game on its computer system and it works, its system will not be identical to yours so this will not be an excuse for the shop to dismiss your claim.

The need for speed

Video games are responsible for driving many advances in computer graphics, as a result of which games players are constantly having to upgrade their kit to be able to play the latest action games. The usual method is to upgrade the graphics card to support more 3D acceleration features. However, increasing memory can improve the speed of video games, as well as overall software performance.

As home users get increasingly faster Internet connections, the first users to exploit the technology are likely to be gamers. Instead of single players battling against the artificial intelligence of a PC, users will play in huge gaming worlds. This type of multi-users' experience is available today, but owing to the complexity of modern games and the slowness of the Internet it is often a frustrating experience. Applications like DirectX are at the heart of much of this Internet gaming.

The two main information panels under the Sound tab give details of the name of the soundcard, the version of the driver which controls the card and whether this hardware has been certified by Microsoft as compatible with DirectX. Using uncertified drivers is not usually a problem; however, you may be able to download newer drivers from your soundcard manufacturer's web site.

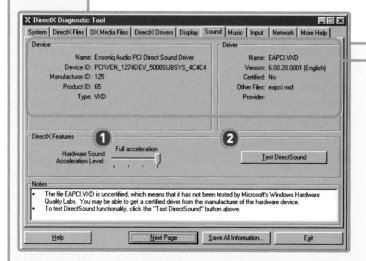

1 Modern soundcards have a form of acceleration that relieves some of the work of your processor and instead allows the soundcard to process information itself. This acceleration can help performance but may cause errors. You can reduce the amount of acceleration with this lever to reduce errors caused by this feature.

2 You can test the various playback qualities and sampling rates using the test DirectSound button. The test will use different features of your soundcard. If some of these settings fail to play make sure you use settings which do work for your games.

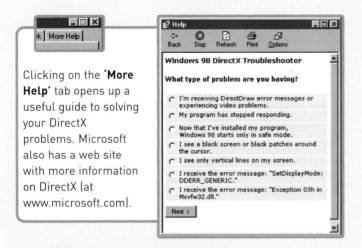

Clicking on the **'More Help'** tab opens up a useful guide to solving your DirectX problems. Microsoft also has a web site with more information on DirectX (at www.microsoft.com).

Sometimes when a game is being played the screen becomes very dark, making it difficult for the player to see the game area. This is because different monitors have varying brightness levels and the game designers are unable to cater for every type of monitor. To change the brightness level, look for a feature called 'gamma correction'. This is normally in either your games options menu or in the graphics card's 'display properties', which can be accessed by right-clicking on the desktop and selecting Properties.

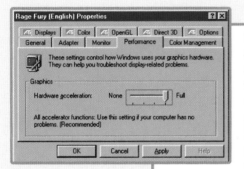

Right-clicking on the desktop and selecting **'Properties'** allows you to change some of the settings of your graphics card. If you experience problems, try reducing hardware acceleration and if possible turning off more of the advanced features of your graphics card. These may include alpha-blending, z-buffering and texture-mapping. Although turning off these features may reduce performance, experimenting with these settings may get a game to work.

Basic troubleshooting | 4

Internet gaming tips

The most common problem that players have is called latency. This is the delay caused by sending and processing game information across the Internet. To help reduce this problem, try using:
- sites based in the UK
- dial-up games services like Gameplay (but they incur additional costs)
- a direct-dial connection, which allows you to connect to another user via a direct telephone call. This often offers the best gaming experience but restricts the number of players to just two
- games that are turn-based, like chess, because they are the easiest to play across the Net and in most cases the software is free. Have a look at www.freeloader.com for a selection of free games.

This section deals with solving more serious PC problems. These problems generally occur when a piece of hardware or software has failed or is producing errors. Before you start getting out screwdrivers and anti-static wrist straps, it is worth checking all the paperwork that came with the system. The standard warranty for a new PC is one year, while many companies offer a five-year labour (not parts) warranty for free. Given that you have already paid for this service as part of the PC's purchase price, getting a properly trained engineer to fix your PC for free is always the best solution.

A word of warning, however: most companies do not consider software problems (even if the software came with the computer) to be their responsibility and may require additional payment to solve these types of problems.

For older, or second-hand, machines, enforcing a warranty agreement may not be possible. Unless you have a very obscure make of PC, almost any of the 5,000+ PC repair specialists in the UK should be able to fix your PC but the labour cost will be quite high. For example, the labour cost of replacing a broken floppy disk drive is often twice the cost of the parts required. Hence, this section covers simple fixes which could save you some painful repair bills.

Thankfully, most errors are caused by software problems and as such can be fixed without the use of screwdrivers or new components. The great skill is understanding the way a machine works and making educated guesses at what the problem might be. No book could cover every possible problem faced by a PC owner and every possible solution. A good tip, however, is to remember, if you are about to change a setting, to note down what it was before you changed it. If the troubleshooting does not work, you can always change it back.

ADVANCED TROUBLESHOOTING

5.1 PC architecture
A fuller description of the PC system.

5.2 The BIOS
The Basic Input Output System.

5.3 PC boot-up examined
What happens when you first turn on your PC and
how this can help with troubleshooting.

5.4 Bootlog
The Bootlog.txt file: a useful tool for the troubleshooter.

5.5 Safe mode
How this special diagnostic mode works.

5.6 Solving software conflicts
Tips for solving more complex software problems.

5.7 Solving hardware conflicts
Tips for solving more complex hardware problems.

5.8 Introducing DOS
What is DOS and how can it help the troubleshooter?

5.9 Re-installing Windows
If a Windows problem cannot be fixed, re-installing it is a
drastic but effective measure.

PC ARCHITECTURE

For advanced troubleshooting on a PC system you need to understand the fundamentals of PC architecture. As in a car's engine, it is all the parts working together which makes the machine run smoothly. Often, when one part is faulty, the problem lies with an interconnecting device used by the system. For example, if a printer does not print, the fault could lie with a software program used by Windows to control the printer, rather than with the printer itself. This section explains PC fundamentals.

The diagram opposite shows the elements of a PC.

Starting up the PC

As the PC is turned on power goes to each hardware device (**keyboard**, **storage mediums**, **RAM** and **processor**) and each in turn is tested by the **BIOS & chipset** on the motherboard.

As each **hardware** device responds, **RAM** (Random Access Memory) is loaded with its settings and a small program to start up **Windows**.

As **Windows** starts it takes the device settings from **RAM** and loads them into the drivers, which make further checks before starting up the **system applications** which may rely on these drivers. Once these **system applications** are started, **Windows** is ready to execute **software applications**.

Using software

When you use a software application, the PC follows a set pattern of activities to accomplish the task. For example, if you are word processing, as you press the A key on the **keyboard**, a signal is sent via the **chipset** to the **resource manager**, which in turn passes on the request to the driver which monitors the **keyboard** for Windows.

This keystroke is passed to the word-processing **application**, which then sends the command for processing to the **processor**, where the application program calculates what to do with the key press.

In our example the word-processing software decides to create the letter A in the chosen position in the document. Another chain of events is started to display this new character. This sequence finally sends the letter A to the **output device**, in this case the **screen**.

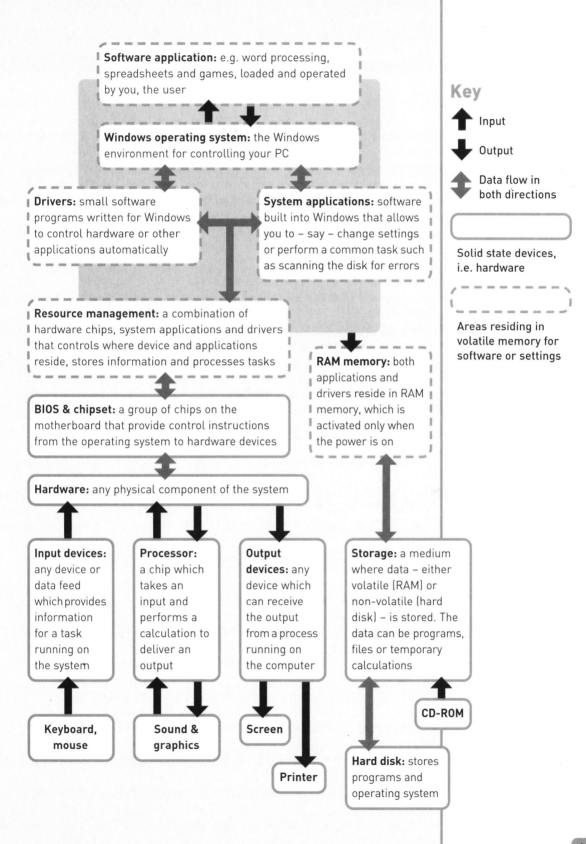

Software application: e.g. word processing, spreadsheets and games, loaded and operated by you, the user

Windows operating system: the Windows environment for controlling your PC

Drivers: small software programs written for Windows to control hardware or other applications automatically

System applications: software built into Windows that allows you to – say – change settings or perform a common task such as scanning the disk for errors

Resource management: a combination of hardware chips, system applications and drivers that controls where device and applications reside, stores information and processes tasks

RAM memory: both applications and drivers reside in RAM memory, which is activated only when the power is on

BIOS & chipset: a group of chips on the motherboard that provide control instructions from the operating system to hardware devices

Hardware: any physical component of the system

Input devices: any device or data feed which provides information for a task running on the system

Processor: a chip which takes an input and performs a calculation to deliver an output

Output devices: any device which can receive the output from a process running on the computer

Storage: a medium where data – either volatile (RAM) or non-volatile (hard disk) – is stored. The data can be programs, files or temporary calculations

Keyboard, mouse

Sound & graphics

Screen

Printer

CD-ROM

Hard disk: stores programs and operating system

Key

Input

Output

Data flow in both directions

Solid state devices, i.e. hardware

Areas residing in volatile memory for software or settings

5 | Advanced troubleshooting

THE BIOS

The Basic Input-Output System (BIOS) is a piece of software on a chip that contains basic settings for most of the major components within your PC. Because the BIOS directly controls your hardware, many of your PC's fundamental settings can be changed only by changing the BIOS. Many different manufacturers produce BIOS chips, to work with different features and settings. Covering each variety of BIOS would fill thousands of pages, but some features are common to every BIOS. This section explains the basic parts of a BIOS.

Warning!

Many Windows utilities contained within the Control Panel are used by other programs. Removing key applications such as 'Dial up networking' may affect Internet and facsimile settings.

The Basic Input-Output System (BIOS)

The first screen of text you see whenever you start up your PC tells you what processor, or CPU (Central Processing Unit), you have and how much RAM is fitted to your PC. This screen may appear fleetingly; pressing down the Pause key should slow it down so you can inspect it closely. The screen also refers to the BIOS. If you press the key that is mentioned at the bottom of the screen – normally Delete, F1 or F2 — you get into the Setup utility, which lets you alter the **BIOS settings**. The BIOS, a special chip burned on to the motherboard, contains software and information about your PC and how to start it up. Its components include the boot-loader, which copies enough information into RAM to allow the PC to start up, and the Power-On Self-Test, which checks that the memory, graphics cards and other elements are working properly.

Main screen

When you arrive at the main screen you will see basic system information, e.g. speed and type of processor and amount of RAM fitted. These are automatically detected and you cannot change the settings but it is a useful check when upgrading RAM or processors. However, you should take a note of the BIOS version. It may be possible to download an update (check the version number against the manufacturer's web site first). The update may enable you to use new features for devices that have been produced since the PC was manufactured.

Basic BIOS options

Before you take a look at your BIOS, you should note that this book provides only broad guidelines. BIOS manufacturers may develop different BIOS for different motherboards, even customising a BIOS for an individual PC manufacturer. But despite the differences of detail, the general principles behind them remain the same.

Drives

You can access some quite advanced options even from the main screen. Your hard disk is probably set to Auto type, and it is best to leave it this way. However, if you set type to User and turn off Logical Block Addressing (a factory preset) you can change some of the size settings. This should be done with extreme caution but might let you squeeze some extra capacity out of an old hard disk.

Time and date

You can change your PC's time and date using this option. Often, the date is in American format. It is probably easier to change the time and date in Windows rather than here.

Boot order

On this Boot screen, you can change the order in which your PC looks for a disk containing system files, which it must find in order to start up. Normally, it will check your floppy drive, then hard disk, then CD-ROM. You can change this order: if you move the floppy drive further down, it will stop anyone starting your machine from a floppy disk (i.e. without having to give a password, thereby bypassing any software security settings).

Ports

Under '**Peripheral Configuration**' (usually on the '**Advanced**' screen) you can change settings for your serial and parallel ports. Memory and Interrupt settings need be changed only to avoid conflicts. A conflict occurs when two devices are trying to use the same IRQ. You can also check the parallel port mode. It should be at least bi-directional, but EPP and ECP are enhanced modes that offer faster data transfer for devices like printers and scanners.

Power management

If you have a separate Power screen, you can control your system's power-saving behaviour. If you enable Power Management Support, your PC will switch off automatically when you tell it to. You can also control whether devices like the system fan, hard disk and screen '**go to sleep**' after a period of inactivity, and how long this should be.

'Wake on LAN/modem ring'

On the Boot screen, you can allow your PC to be switched on automatically by certain events such as activity on the Local Area Network (LAN) or, for home users, the arrival of a fax.

Password (security)

You may have a separate Security screen, or this option may appear on the main screen. It is possible to set a user password to control access to your PC, and a supervisor password to control access to these BIOS screens. You need to type each twice: don't forget these passwords, as without your BIOS password you will not able to start the system or change BIOS settings.

Cache

You can turn memory cache on or off from the Advanced screen. This is a super-fast type of memory which speeds up your PC by storing frequently used instructions for quick access. '**Cache ECC support**' is an option you can select for error correction: turning it on slows your PC very slightly but checks the cache for errors and improves reliability.

Event logging

Event logging can keep a check on any problems faced by your system as it boots up. Many of these sound worse than they really are – e.g. a stuck key can produce a '**dead keyboard error**' – but it can be interesting to keep an eye on them. If the event log produces an increasing number of problems, you may have an intermittent hardware fault with memory or your hard disk.

Advanced BIOS features

If you go to the Advanced screen and choose '**Resource Configuration**' you can change settings which nowadays it is better to alter through Windows System Properties. However, if old expansion cards cause trouble, it may be useful to allocate them specific areas of memory or particular IRQs here (see Glossary for more on IRQs). Do this only in conjunction with the card's documentation.

PC BOOT-UP EXAMINED

When a PC is turned on, the system performs many tasks before the Windows operating system starts. This process is called booting. When Windows fails to start correctly or reports errors constantly, these problems can be fixed by altering the boot-up process. This section explains how a boot-up works and how to correct problems that may occur during the boot-up phase.

BIOS tests hardware:
memory, floppy disk, keyboard, hard disk

If a fault occurs during the BIOS test, the BIOS generates an error message. This message may indicate hardware problems, such as a loose connection, failed component or incorrect settings in the BIOS.

Autoexec.bat runs, **Config.sys** runs

The Autoexec.bat and Config.sys files load DOS programs into the memory before Windows loads. These are typically anti-virus programs or security software. Removing these applications (which may be corrupt or causing errors) can help a successful boot.

Applications in Startup group run

The Startup group loads applications which have been set to run automatically. If these applications are causing errors, Windows may fail to start. See section 2.10 for tips on managing the Startup group.

Boot sector
loads command.com

The boot sector is a special part of the disk which contains instructions for loading the operating system into the computer's memory. This boot sector can get corrupted. See opposite for how to fix this problem.

Windows checks to see if hardware has changed and is working. If hardware o.k., load hardware drivers. Next load system applications, such as start bar, desktop and fonts.

As Windows boots, it makes a rudimentary check on all the hardware and software it believes is installed. If these checks are passed, Windows continues. If not, it automatically tries to fix any problems. If the problems are unfixable, Windows may crash during this phase. Using the safe mode (see section 5.5) can help with troubleshooting.

Fixing a corrupted boot sector

The boot sector is the most important part of the hard disk because without it the computer cannot start up correctly. The boot sector, like any part of a computer hard disk, is susceptible to data corruption through wear and tear.

Section 2.4 explained how to create a **'Windows Recovery disk'** on a floppy disk. From this disk you can often fix a corrupted boot sector on the hard-disk drive.

If your PC fails to boot and shows the message **'Unable to load command.com'** or **'Drive not ready'** try these simple troubleshooting steps:
• make sure no floppy disk is in the drive and restart your PC
• examine the BIOS to make sure the primary hard-disk drive is still listed (see section 5.2)
• try booting into safe mode (see section 5.5).

If all these fixes fail, insert your recovery disk and restart your PC. If the computer starts now, it should display the **'A:'** prompt. Now type:

SYS C:

and press return. Wait until the message **'System transferred'** appears, remove the disk and restart the computer. The system should now at least start, although if you have had boot-sector corruption you may have additional problems to contend with.

If the system fails to start from the recovery disk:
• check that the BIOS has the correct boot sequence (see section 5.2)
• test the recovery disk on another PC, to make sure it too is not corrupted
• try using the recovery disk created by your anti-virus software, as some viruses can prevent successful booting.

BOOTLOG

During the boot-up process, Windows creates a useful file called bootlog.txt that is stored on the hard disk after boot-up. This file provides information about which hardware devices and software drivers have installed. With this data you can take action to fix problems. This section explains how to examine bootlog.txt for indications of problems.

To view the bootlog file, which is normally hidden, you first need to make visible all hidden files. Double-click on My Computer and then double-click on the C: drive. On the main menu of this drive, select **'View'**, **'Folder Options'**, **'View'**, then make sure that the **'Show all files'** button is selected under the hidden files attribute.

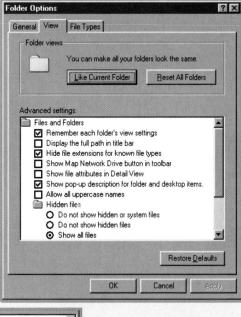

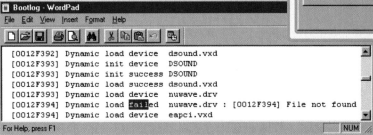

If you now look back in the main C: drive you will see some additional files. If you double-click on the file called **'bootlog.txt'** it will load this file into the basic Windows word processor (Wordpad). This file has thousands of lines of information, describing what happened during the last Windows boot-up, including whether each hardware and Windows device installed correctly. If the device loaded correctly, the word **'success'** will appear next to the device. If there was a problem, the word **'failed'** will appear instead. In the example above, the nuwave.drv has failed to load because Windows could not find the file. To find out what this device is used for we need to search the hard drive for references to nuwave. In this case nuwave is the soundcard driver, which has been accidentally deleted.

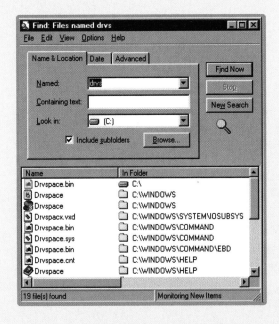

By using WordPad's built-in search utility, you can search bootlog for instances when a device failed. To use this feature press Ctrl+F, then type Fail as the search string. Each time you press the F3 key it will search for another failed device. Some devices' drivers always fail; in many cases this is not the sign of an error but simply part of the boot-up process. For example, many bootlogs contain this line:

LoadFailed = C:\WINDOWS\COMMAND\DRVSPACE.SYS

To find out more about the file which has failed you need to locate it and examine its properties. To locate it, start up the Find File utility (see section 2.9) and enter the first part of the file name without the extension (see below).

Now, right-click on any of these files to examine their properties. In this case the file which has failed is the built-in drive compression utility (see section 2.8). It failed because there are no compressed drives on the system so the device did not load. This is normal — not an error.

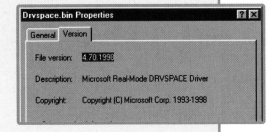

If you follow the steps described above for each failed file you can find what has failed and what hardware or software it correlates to. This is a process of deduction: e.g. if you are experiencing problems with a creative lab's soundcard and a file called creativeSc.drv located in the C:\Creative\Directory has failed to load, this may indicate that the driver is corrupted or the incorrect version. The driver version must match both its associated hardware and your version of Windows.

SAFE MODE

Windows safe mode is a special way of starting the Windows operating system when errors prevent it starting in the normal way. When in safe mode, many of Windows' more advanced functions are disabled, which allows you to perform permanent fixes to errant applications and Windows features. This section covers how to get to the Windows safe mode and how to use it to fix problems.

Entering safe mode

To enter safe mode, press the F8 key as your PC boots up. At this point you are presented with an options menu. Here, select **'Safe mode'** and Windows will begin to boot.

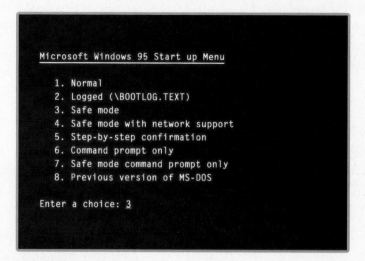

```
Microsoft Windows 95 Start up Menu

    1. Normal
    2. Logged (\BOOTLOG.TEXT)
    3. Safe mode
    4. Safe mode with network support
    5. Step-by-step confirmation
    6. Command prompt only
    7. Safe mode command prompt only
    8. Previous version of MS-DOS

Enter a choice: 3
```

Limitations of safe mode

Safe mode is a good way to determine whether a Windows problem is driver-related. The logic is that if it boots in safe mode, which has very few drivers loaded, you can then start removing system tasks until Windows boots again normally.

Safe mode has its limitations:
• you cannot install applications in safe mode
• some applications may not work in safe mode
• many devices won't work in safe mode.

Safe mode is a good way to get files off your system in an emergency, if Windows won't start correctly.

Common problems that can be fixed in safe mode:

• if you have set a screen resolution which garbles your screen, safe mode resets your screen drivers back to a known good setting. From here you can select a resolution which is suitable and then restart your machine
• if you have installed a program in the start-up group which is now stopping Windows from starting, safe mode ignores this group and allows you to remove this program
• if your hardware has been upgraded and is now stopping Windows from starting, safe mode loads minimal driver support and allows device drivers to be removed
• if an application crashes when the uninstall routine is started, you can uninstall it in safe mode.

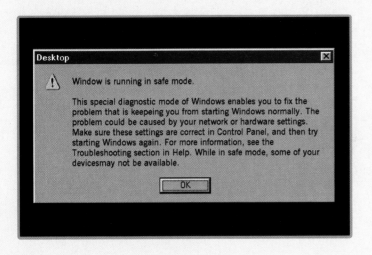

SOLVING SOFTWARE CONFLICTS

Solving more complex errors, especially if you are trying to get two applications to work together, can be quite difficult. Applications which try to take control of a Windows resource such as a soundcard or parallel port all for themselves may not be fixable. Such programs have to be used separately. This section suggests some more advanced methods of resolving software conflicts.

Even when Windows first loads, several programs may already be running in the background, performing essential Windows tasks or functions at the request of the user. Common background tasks include anti-virus software, graphics-card utilities and media players.

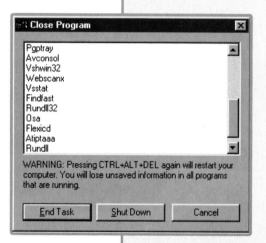

Sometimes an application stops working or crashes the moment it is started. One possible cause is that another application is conflicting with its operation.

One possible solution is to shut down other applications to get the errant application to work. To shut down an application, simply press Ctrl +Alt + Delete simultaneously, select the task and click on the **'End Task'** button. Before you start shutting down a running task, check which other tasks are running.

By using the Windows System Information utility (see section 4.3) and by looking under the **'Software Environment'** attribute, you can find out which applications are currently running on your system. From here you can choose which applications to suspend in order to resolve a conflict. As a rule of thumb, any applications listed as part of the Microsoft Windows operating system should be left alone.

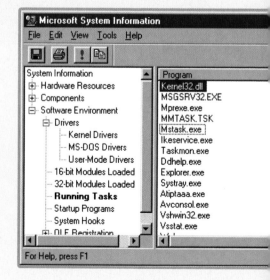

Possible solutions

• Fax software often conflicts with connecting to the Internet.
Shutting down the fax client can resolve this.
• Special software for controlling advanced joysticks can
hamper the operation of MIDI devices like music keyboards.
• Drivers for parallel port scanners can sometimes affect other
parallel port devices such as Zip drives.
• If the version of the software of a driver is old it may not be
compatible with newer applications or Windows versions. Check
the web site of the software manufacturer for a later version.
• Some tasks require another application to be loaded before
they will work. A joystick driver may require the correct
soundcard drivers to be installed before the joystick will work.
• Some devices take control of a port even if the device is no
longer attached. A good example of this is software for a
personal organiser which allows files to be copied between the
desktop PC and the portable device. Even if the device is not
attached, the software may still retain control of the serial ports.

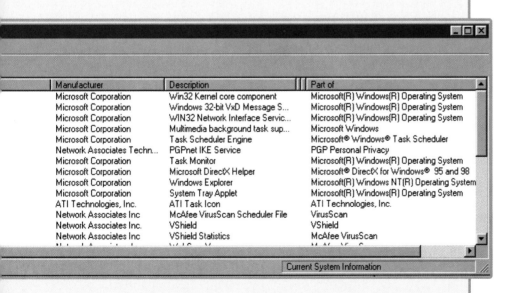

SOLVING HARDWARE CONFLICTS

When a new PC is built, it is very unlikely that the accompanying hardware and software will conflict. But as new hardware is added to the system or software is changed or removed, hardware devices such as scanners, soundcards and modems may start to go wrong owing to hardware conflicts. This section covers the more advanced methods of testing and fixing hardware errors.

Windows warnings

 This symbol may appear next to a device: it means that Windows believes that the driver is not working correctly. Unless you notice a problem, this can indicate that the driver is not entirely compatible but the device is still working.

 A red cross through a device indicates that it has either been disabled by the user or has not been configured properly. Some devices, such as external scanners or digital cameras, may display this symbol if turned off, when the PC is first booted up.

? A yellow question mark denotes a device that Windows does not recognise. This is not always an error as some devices talk directly to the hardware, circumventing Windows.

Modern hardware devices use a system called **'plug and play'** to solve the problem of dividing up system resources such as memory and IRQ (see glossary). Before 'plug and play', devices often had to be set up manually to prevent them from getting confused or trying to use each other's resources.

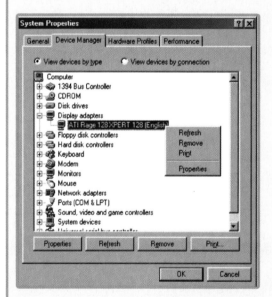

On a modern desktop PC running Windows it is very unlikely that hardware conflicts will occur, but as you add more and more devices to your PC, problems could arise. The typical result of a conflict is that a device stops working or an error occurs when two devices are working at the same time.

Conflicts also occur during upgrading. Some devices need to use very specific resources and will block any other device from using that resource. To resolve this type of problem, remove the device and let Windows find it again and reassign resources to it. When Windows attempts to reload the device it will try to allocate resources taking into account any other devices currently running. To remove a device, open the System Properties Window (see section 1.10) and remove the offending device by right-clicking on it and selecting **'Remove'**. If you now restart Windows, it should detect the device, re-install the drivers and try to find the best settings for it.

If re-installing the device does not work, you may have to change the driver's settings or change the driver for a newer version.

Each device has a general information screen, containing manufacturer and version details.

Some devices have additional information and configuration tabs.

In this case, the status tab is available. Once it is selected, more detailed information about the device becomes available. This is useful for cataloguing your system and for deciding whether you need to upgrade a device driver.

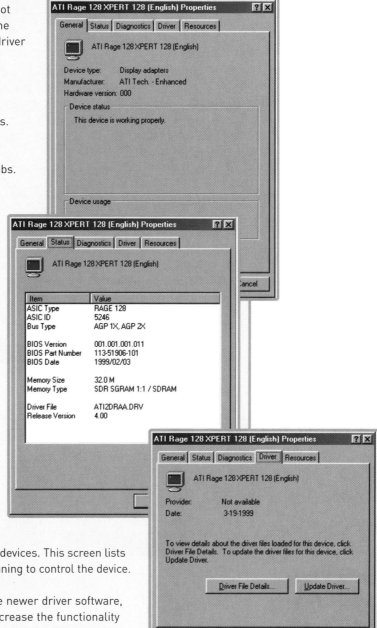

The driver tab is available for all devices. This screen lists the software that Windows is running to control the device.

PC manufacturers often produce newer driver software, either to fix known bugs or to increase the functionality of a device. In this example, the driver for this graphics card was released in March 1999; as the system is working correctly, there is no need to apply an update.

Updates for drivers are often available from the web site of the device manufacturer. Simply download a new driver and follow the instructions supplied by the hardware manufacturer (installation instructions vary depending on the device and manufacturer).

INTRODUCING DOS

On most PCs Windows has replaced the Disk Operating System (DOS). However, some older software, including some games and financial programs, still uses DOS. Some DOS programs work erratically with Windows but software companies may provide lower-cost or occasionally free upgrades to versions suitable for Windows.

Getting to DOS

Method 1 Either use the programs menu or click on **'Start'**, then **'Restart in MS-DOS mode'**, to begin a DOS session. This is the simplest way of getting to DOS; if, however, you want to use older DOS programs, Method 2 is likely to be more successful.

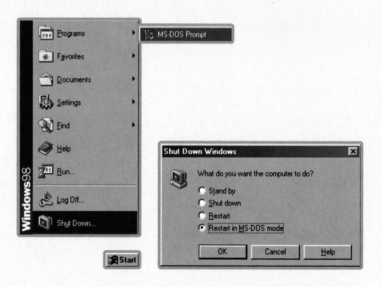

Warning!

If you are in DOS mode, always go back to Windows and select 'Shutdown' before turning off the machine.

Method 2 Pressing the F8 key when you start your machine brings up a menu that gives you the option to start MS-DOS. This method often prevents soundcards and CD-ROM drives from functioning correctly.

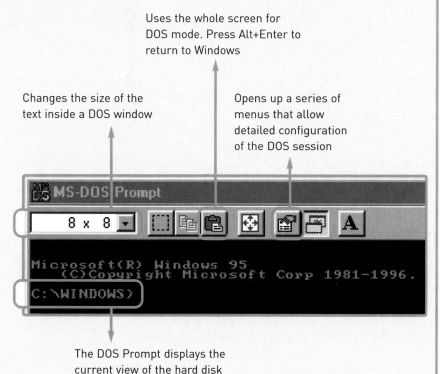

Uses the whole screen for DOS mode. Press Alt+Enter to return to Windows

Changes the size of the text inside a DOS window

Opens up a series of menus that allow detailed configuration of the DOS session

The DOS Prompt displays the current view of the hard disk

Simple words

Most versions of Windows come with a simple text editor. Just go to the DOS prompt and type EDIT. Use the Alt key to access the software's menus.

Simple DOS commands

CD C:\WINDOWS This command moves the current view to the Windows directory on the **C:** hard disk. (CD = change directory)

CD IMAGES\CLIPART In this instance the current view moves to the Images\Clipart directory.

CD D: This variation changes the current view to the **D:** drive.

CD:\.. This is a special command that takes you back to the main directory for the drive.

DIR /P This command lists all the files and directories at the current location, **P**ausing after every page.

DIR C:\LETTER.DOC/S/P This command looks across the whole of the **C:** drive for a file called **LETTER**, which is a **DOC**ument. The search will check all **S**ubdirectories while **P**ausing after every page has been listed to the screen.

EXIT Typing **'exit'** returns you to Windows.

SOS! DOS to the rescue

If you have a major problem with your PC and Windows will not start, DOS will allow the basic recovery of files. Using the Copy command, you can move important files over from the hard disk to floppy disk. Typing the command COPY C:\BUDGET.XLS A:\ will copy an Excel spreadsheet entitled 'Budget' from the C: hard disk on to a floppy disk. To find out more about the copy command, type COPY /? at the DOS prompt.

RE-INSTALLING WINDOWS

If you have a major problem with Windows and you have tried every possible solution, including speaking to the PC manufacturer, without success, sometimes the only solution is to re-install Windows. This section takes you through the steps involved.

Re-installing Windows is quite a drastic step. It falls into two categories: re-installing Windows over an existing version, or erasing everything on the system and re-loading the Windows operating system, device drivers and software applications. Before you re-install Windows make sure you move your documents to a directory on the main root (i.e. on the C: drive), so that they will be unaffected by the process.

1 The easiest way to re-install Windows is to place the original Windows CD-ROM in the drive and the Windows Startup disk (see section 2.4) in the floppy drive and restart your system. The machine will now boot and prompt you to start the installation procedure.

2 Another method is to start the Windows setup procedure from within Windows by using the **'Find'** command (see section 2.9) to locate the Setup.exe file — often located in C:\windows\options\cabs — and then double-click on it.

3 The third method is to start the PC and, when the words **'Starting Windows'** appear, press the F8 key. This will bring up a special menu from which you need to select the **'Safe mode command prompt'**.

No matter which option you use, you need your registration number (on the **'certificate of authenticity'** which accompanied your PC), which means you have a legal version of the software and entitles you to technical support from Microsoft. If you do not have this, contact your PC dealer.

If you have re-installed Windows over an existing version and the system is still problematic, you can re-install Windows from scratch. This requires a bit more planning.

You will need your original Windows installation CD and all the device drivers for the hardware on your PC, which should have been supplied by your PC manufacturer on either a CD or a collection of floppy disks.

Any applications such as word processing which came with your PC should also be available on CD-ROM. Your PC manufacturer has a legal requirement to supply these.

A boot (start-up) disk should have been created when you first got your machine (see section 2.4). If you don't have a boot disk, you can make one on another PC with the same operating system. Then:

1 place the boot disk in the PC and restart the system

2 place the Windows CD-ROM in the drive and follow the instructions that accompany the installation CD

3 as Windows installs, if it can't find any system drivers it will ask you to supply the relevant driver disk

4 test your PC by running simple applications and saving files. If the system now appears to be stable, install your main software application.

This method of re-installing Windows tries to use your old installation as a basis for installing the new version. If your old version is very unstable you may need to delete it before re-installing Windows again. To do this you need to add an extra step between steps 1 and 2:

• after rebooting the system, use the DOS directory command (see section 5.8) to locate the Windows directory. This is normally found as **C:\Windows** or **C:\Win98**. When you locate this directory you need to delete it (to do so, at the C:\ prompt, type: **Deltree (name of the directory)/s**. The Deltree command is very powerful and will delete all of the Windows directory and associated settings files. If you have any documents within the Windows directory, these will also be deleted. You might want to use the DOS commands in section 5.8 to move these files to another directory before you run Deltree. Now proceed to step 2.

This method is more drastic because if you do not have all the drivers for your system on your Windows CD-ROM, you will have to either contact your PC manufacturer or search on its web site for the drivers.

One reason why the PC is such a powerful machine is its potential for being upgraded. Most upgrades can be carried out by the user, but the huge variety of different PC designs and configurations can sometimes make even the simplest upgrade tricky.

All new hardware comes with the manufacturer's installation instructions and details of the system requirements for the new piece of kit. These specifications focus on the amount of RAM, type of operating system, the make and model of the processor and what other components are within the computer. The manufacturer will also indicate what free slots within the chassis or on the motherboard the new device will need before it can be installed successfully.

Before you upgrade or install any new devices, check whether your PC matches the required specification. Most of this can be gleaned from the system information screens (see section 1) but sometimes the only way to find out if your PC has the required bays or slots is to look inside the case. If the specification is o.k., read this section's generic instructions for upgrading the part in question, but be aware that they may not be suitable for all types of product, and **always follow the manufacturer's instructions**.

Many upgrades, especially those involving external USB, Parallel or SCSI devices, are very simple, needing only the correct software to carry them out. For other upgrades you need to plug a new card into the computer's motherboard and then run the software. Upgrading a motherboard or a processor is more difficult and could damage the PC if done incorrectly, so these types of upgrades are best left to trained experts, not least because many PC manufacturers deliberately omit instructions for such upgrades.

The dangers of working inside the PC
The PC is an electrical device. If you try to open it while it is still switched on, you risk a fatal shock. Also, the static electric charge we all carry in our bodies can ruin the sensitive electronic components within the computer and/or its peripherals.

UPGRADING AND REPLACING HARDWARE

6.1 Upgrading RAM
More memory improves performance: this section explains how to add it.

6.2 Adding a hard-disk drive
How to add more disk space, for storing files and software.

6.3 Upgrading your graphics system
How to take advantage of new developments in graphics technology.

6.4 Replacing a CD-ROM drive
Upgrading to a CD writer or DVD or replacing a faulty CD-ROM drive.

6.5 Replacing a floppy-disk drive
How to replace a faulty drive.

6.6 Upgrading your sound system
How to install a new soundcard.

6.7 Upgrading your modem
How to upgrade your modem for improved Internet connectivity.

6.8 Replacing a hard-disk drive (I)
The hard disk can fail or simply become inadequate for your needs: this section explains how to upgrade it.

6.9 Replacing a hard-disk drive (II)
More on upgrading a hard disk.

6.10 FAQs on upgrading
Frequently asked questions on upgrading.

TOOLS OF THE TRADE

Most PCs are made to be easily serviceable. Simple cross-head (Phillips) and flat-head screwdrivers are all you will need in most cases.

Some PC manufacturers use special security screws to prevent tampering or to secure components with no serviceable parts such as power supplies or the insides of hard disks.

To protect yourself and your PC

- Always switch the PC off, and then turn it off at the wall, but leave it plugged in – this will ensure that the PC chassis remains earthed.

- Before touching any components, always touch a metal part of the PC chassis to discharge any static harmlessly. Ideally, buy an anti-static wristband and connect this to the PC whenever you are working on it to ensure that you remain earthed and cannot build up a static charge.

- Never open up the power supply. Because it is a transformer, even when it is switched off it can carry high residual voltages. If it is faulty, replace the entire unit: there are no user-serviceable parts inside (the same applies to monitors).

- Do not open up your screen: doing this could mean a deadly shock.

- When working with chips, try not to touch any of the pins or connectors: these carry any static shock right to the heart of the chip, burning out transistors.

UPGRADING RAM

Where to buy RAM

Many computer upgrade centres offer free fitting for memory purchased from them. This avoids possible incompatibilities and is often a 'while you wait' service, although it is more expensive than buying RAM via mail order.

Warning!

Memory is very sensitive to static electricity, so you should always take anti-static precautions before you remove or replace memory sticks (see also page 133).

- Ensure the PC is still plugged in to the mains power but the wall socket is turned off.

- Touch the fingers of both hands on a metal part of the PC chassis to remove static electricity from your body before handling any memory modules.

Random Access Memory (RAM) is essential for the operation of your PC. Adding more RAM to your system – a relatively simple upgrade – can improve the performance of every aspect of your machine. This section covers how to identify the type of memory you need to buy and how to fit it into your system safely.

Knowing what memory to buy

Most new PCs tend to be sold with 32Mb or 64Mb of RAM pre-installed. For simple tasks such as word processing, Internet access and home finance, this is generally sufficient. If multiple applications are running and Windows needs more RAM, it uses the hard disk as a form of slower ('virtual') memory. Applications involving graphics or video tend to be more RAM-hungry, as do many 3D games or multimedia programs. The types and cost of memory are constantly changing; as a rule, RAM memory costs £1–£2 per megabyte and is normally available in 32, 64 and 128Mb units. PCs from different manufacturers often use different types of memory depending on performance, motherboard architecture and cost. So before rushing out to buy new memory, you need to find out two important things.

What type of memory does your PC use?

Memory comes in several different configurations defining physical size and speed. The manufacturer of your machine can give you the information about your PC. If this assistance is not available, removing a memory stick from your machine (open the chassis of the computer, find the PC memory slots – see example below – and pull out a stick) and taking it to a local computer centre for identification is another option. Before removing memory, make sure you follow the anti-static precautions detailed on the left and on page 133.

How many free memory slots are available?

PC memory sits in dedicated slots on the system motherboard. Each of these slots can accept one memory stick, with the total amount of memory not exceeding the motherboard's upper limit. Most PCs accept at least 384Mb of RAM (i.e. 3 x 128Mb), although more advanced systems can support up to 1,024Mb (i.e. 4 x 256Mb.). Open the chassis of the computer, find the PC memory slots (see diagrams 2 and 3 opposite) and count how many free slots you have. You should also note if the memory stick has chips on both sides of the module, as it is always advisable to find memory that matches in this respect.

2

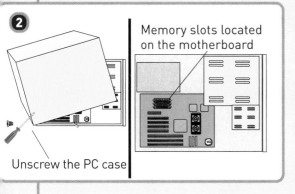

Memory slots located on the motherboard

Unscrew the PC case

3

Note the direction of the existing memory stick before inserting the new one

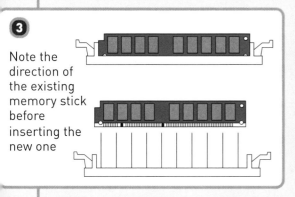

4

Screw the case back on to the PC

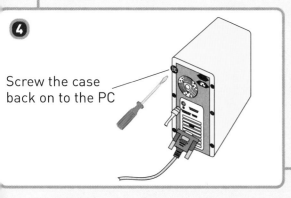

How to add RAM

1 Turn the power off at the mains and take anti-static precautions (see opposite margin).

2 Open the chassis and locate the free memory slots. These may be obscured by cables or the hard drive.

3 Locate the existing memory sticks, match up the new memory in the same direction, slide the new stick into the slot and click it into place. The memory will go in only one way. If you have to force it, try it the other way.

4 Secure the PC's chassis and reconnect the monitor, keyboard, mouse and power cables. Restart the system.

5 When the machine boots up it should automatically detect the new memory, providing an increased total. You can confirm this by right clicking on the 'My Computer' icon within Windows and selecting 'Properties'.

Memory management

The Windows operating system can be speeded up greatly by additional memory. This is often a way of avoiding costly and complex processor or motherboard upgrades. Memory also has a long life span and can be moved from older PCs to newer systems provided the basic memory type is the same. The most common type of memory is DIMMs (Dual Inline Memory Modules), which are found in 85 per cent of all desktop PCs capable of supporting Windows 98.

What to do if the upgrade does not work

Power down the system and open up the chassis. Make sure that all the memory sticks are firmly in place. Then restart the computer.

If even that does not work, remove an existing memory stick and put the new memory in its slot. Restart the system and see if the PC recognises the new memory. If it does, try the old memory in a slot directly adjacent to the new one. If the PC fails to recognise the old memory, you have memory of differing types and need to contact your memory supplier.

ADDING A HARD-DISK DRIVE

Before you start

Check your PC warranty. This task is quite time-consuming and there may be aspects of the design of your PC that affect the way an upgrade must be carried out. Most PC vendors provide experts on a technical support phone line to advise on such matters. If you are unsure, consult these experts before you begin.

Warning!

The main source of danger when working inside a PC is electricity. To protect yourself and your PC, take the following steps (see also page 133).

● Ensure the PC is still plugged in to the mains power but the wall socket is turned off.

● Touch the fingers of both hands on a metal part of the PC chassis to remove static electricity from your body before touching any components.

The software on your system resides on the hard disk. Most PC systems can hold more than one hard disk, thereby allowing you to store more software and data files. Hard-disk drives are getting progressively faster, such that new ones are often much faster than those made just a year or two previously. The detailed procedures for fitting a second hard-disk drive vary from one machine to the next. Follow the manufacturer's instructions in the context of this section's advice.

As computer applications (especially games) grow in size, you may need more space on your hard disk (see section 2.8). Instead of replacing your hard disk (see sections 6.8 and 6.9), you can add a second hard disk. But first make sure that the computer's chassis can support another drive.

● Open the chassis and find the existing hard disk, which will be located in a housing inside the PC secured by four screws. See if the chassis has an empty housing of a similar size which a second drive can fit into.

● Check whether the ribbon cable leading from the current hard drive to the motherboard has an additional plug on it, so it can connect to a second drive. If it does not, buy a new cable with a second connector in the middle (see diagram).

● Find out if you have enough power connectors free inside the chassis to support a second drive. Locate your existing hard drive and the power cable (see diagram), then find a matching unused cable. Also test that this power cable will reach your new hard disk. If you do not have a free power cable, buy an additional power cable splitter.

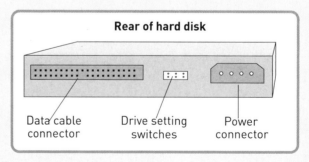

Rear of hard disk

Data cable connector   Drive setting switches   Power connector

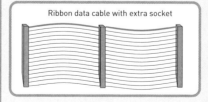

Ribbon data cable with extra socket

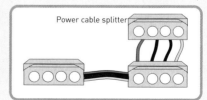

Power cable splitter

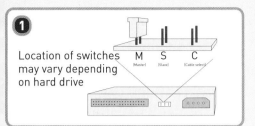

Location of switches
may vary depending
on hard drive

M   S   C
(Master)   (Slave)   (Cable select)

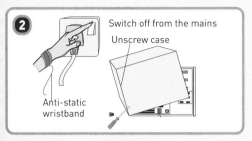

Switch off from the mains

Unscrew case

Anti-static
wristband

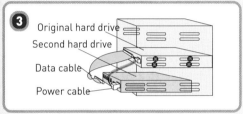

Original hard drive
Second hard drive

Data cable

Power cable

1 Following the steps in the manual for the new hard-disk drive, set the switches at the back (or underside) of the drive for use as a second drive. This is called 'slave' mode, as the second drive will be 'slaved' to the first.

2 Turn the power off at the mains and take anti-static precautions (see margin).

3 Open the chassis, fit the second drive into the free housing and secure with screws. Locate the existing hard disk and run the extra socket on the data cable to the new drive. Be sure to fit the power cable before closing and securing the chassis.

1 Normal
2 Logged
3 Safe mode
4 Step by step confirmation
5 Command prompt only
6 Safe mode command prompt only
7 Previous version of MSDOS

C:\fdisk

1. Create DOS partition or Logical DOS Drive
2. Set active partition
3. Delete partition or Logical DOS drive
4. Display partition information

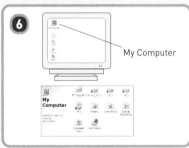

My Computer

4 As your PC restarts, press the F5 key and select MS-DOS mode. From this DOS screen (represented by a C:\) you can partition (see right margin) your drive for use. To set a partition, type 'FDISK' and follow the on-screen instructions. From this screen you can set up more than one virtual drive on each disk. Be careful not to create a partition on the C (i.e. original) drive (called 'drive 1') as you will erase all the information on it.

5 To format the disk, type 'FORMAT (partition letter):'. The partition letter should generally be greater than E because A to D are normally used by floppy, hard disk and CD-ROM drives. Again, do not format the C drive as this is your original drive.

What to do if the new drive does not work

Check that the data and power cables are secured and the right way round. Try swapping the data cable around and go back to step 4 above. Look in the BIOS (see section 5.2) and make sure that the computer has auto-detected the new hard-disk drive. If not, you will need to enter the drive settings as detailed in the manual that came with the drive, or contact your supplier.

6 After the formatting is complete, reboot your PC. Windows should now list the new drive. Check this by double-clicking on the 'My Computer' icon, which lists the available drives.

Partitioning disks

If you have a particularly large hard disk, setting up multiple partitions is useful for organising the files and applications on your PC.

You can use one partition for the Windows system, one for applications and another for data files. This means you can back up just your valuable data files without wasting backup capacity on applications which you already have on CD-ROM.

UPGRADING YOUR GRAPHICS SYSTEM

Before you start

Before you start to upgrade your graphics card, consult your PC warranty. There may be aspects of the design of your PC that affect the way an upgrade must be carried out. Most PC vendors provide experts on a technical support phone line to advise on such matters. If you are unsure, consult them before you begin.

Warning!

The main source of danger when working inside a PC is electricity. To protect yourself and your PC, take the following steps (see also page 133).

- Ensure the PC is still plugged in to the mains power but the wall socket is turned off.

- Touch the fingers of both hands on a metal part of the PC chassis to remove static electricity from your body before touching any components.

The deluge of 3D education, entertainment, design and games software means that graphics card technology can quickly fall from cutting-edge to run-of-the-mill. Replacing your graphics card with the most up-to-date version is a relatively easy task. Follow the manufacturer's instructions in the context of this section's advice.

There are two types of graphics system. The more common one uses an interface slot (or PCI slot) built into the motherboard. The other kind, found in some advanced systems, has a special slot called the AGP (accelerated graphics port), designed only for graphics cards. On lower-cost or business-orientated PCs, the graphics features are embedded on to the motherboard. This makes the PC simpler to manufacture and set up, but hinders upgrading. Before upgrading your video graphics system, decide what type of card best suits your needs and the constraints of your PC. Some are designed for fast-paced, 3D video games, while others are more suited to video editing or CAD. Also, check what types of slots are available for your upgrade.

By accessing the Windows **'Properties'** screen you can find many details about your graphics system before opening the chassis. Look for the amount of video RAM installed and the make and model of the card, to help you decide which type of card to upgrade to. More video memory can speed up performance of all graphic-intensive applications and games. Compare the make and model with another from the same supplier to ascertain what performance gain can be achieved.

To check that the new graphics card is suitable for your PC, open the chassis and locate your existing graphics system by tracing the monitor socket to either a plug-in card or the motherboard. If the graphics system is on the motherboard it probably cannot be upgraded. If the graphics system is on a card, find out if it uses an AGP or PCI slot. AGP slots are slightly smaller.

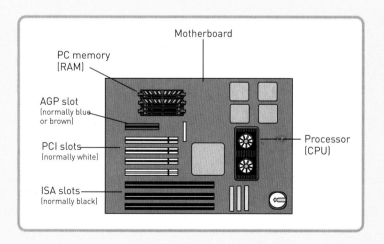

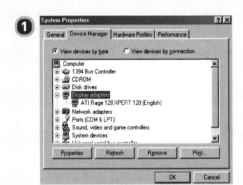

Upgrading a graphics card

1 Go into the 'System Properties' screen in Windows (see section 1.10), remove the existing graphics driver. Then power the system down.

2 Turn the power off at the mains and take anti-static precautions (see opposite margin).

3 Open the chassis and remove the existing graphics card. A single screw normally holds this in place.

4 Insert the new card into the slot, making sure it is secure. If it will not slide in smoothly, check that the card matches the slot. Once inserted, screw the card into place and secure the chassis.

5 Reconnect all the cables and restart your PC. Windows should now detect a new graphics card and ask for the driver disk supplied by the graphics-card manufacturer. The system may need to restart before it will work with the new card.

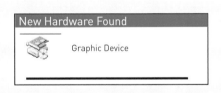

New Hardware Found

Graphic Device

More than a pretty picture

Many modern graphics cards are equipped for more than just PC images. A common feature is to allow television or video signals to be displayed on a PC screen while other applications are also running. This provision for video is also useful for video editing and playing DVD movie disks on your PC. Technically, if you watch TV on your PC screen you need a TV licence.

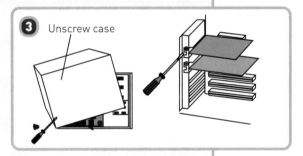

❸ Unscrew case

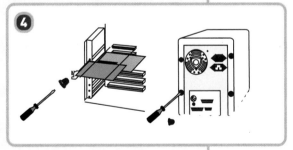

❹

If you turn the computer back on after installing the new card and nothing appears on the screen:

- open the case and make sure that the card is seated securely
- make sure that the monitor cable is also securely fastened to the new graphics card output port
- if you have a graphics card built on to the motherboard, try connecting the monitor to this socket instead. If the display is still active, enter the BIOS (see section 5.2) and disable the onboard graphics.

REPLACING A CD-ROM DRIVE

Before you start

Check your PC warranty. Although the task itself is relatively easy, there may be aspects of the design of your PC that affect the way an upgrade must be carried out. Most PC vendors provide experts on a technical support phone line to advise on such matters. If you are unsure, consult these experts before you begin.

Warning!

The main source of danger when working inside a PC is electricity. To protect yourself and your PC, take the following steps (see also page 133).

- Ensure the PC is still plugged in to the mains power but the wall socket is turned off.

- Touch the fingers of both hands on a metal part of the PC chassis to remove static electricity from your body before touching any components.

Like any electronic device, a CD-ROM drive has a finite life span. This section shows how to test the drive on your PC. If you need to replace it, follow the manufacturer's instructions in the context of this section's advice.

New CD-ROM drives access data at up to 32 times the speed of earlier drives. To upgrade your CD-ROM drive, follow steps 1 to 9 below. If you believe that it has stopped working, try the following procedures before replacing it:

- make sure that the disk is the right way up and seated correctly
- use a CD-ROM disk which is known to work on another computer. If this disk works on your PC, it may be that you have a scratch on the disk you tried originally, not a faulty drive
- make sure that the device is listed in 'System Properties' (see section 1.10) and that Windows believes it to be working
- play an audio disk. If this works it is more likely to be a software – rather than a hardware – problem
- clean the drive with a CD cleaner disk.

If after all these tests you find you need to replace the drive, you will need:

- a new internal IDE or SCSI (see Glossary) CD-ROM drive. These cost £40–£80 and are available from most computer stores. Most desktop PCs use IDE drives, but some powerful systems use SCSI drives
- CD-ROM driver software, which comes with new drives on a floppy disk. If you are buying a second-hand drive, make sure to ask the seller for the driver software disk. Drivers are available on the Internet but can be hard to locate.

How to install a CD-ROM drive

These installation steps cover IDE CD-ROMs as they are the more common type.

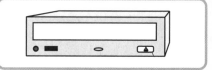

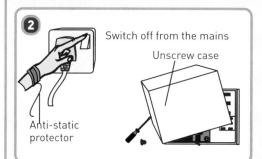

Switch off from the mains

Unscrew case

Anti-static protector

1 In Windows, go to the 'System Information' (see section 1.10) screen and remove the old CD-ROM device. Then power the system down.

2 Turn the power off at the mains and take anti-static precautions (see margin).

3 Open the chassis and locate the cables which run from the motherboard to the rear of the CD-ROM drive. Remove the larger, ribbon-style cable from the back of the drive, taking note of which way up it fitted into the drive.

4 Trace the second, smaller cable which runs from the CD-ROM drive to the power supply. This power cable carries 12v and fits in only one way. Remove this cable from the back of the drive.

5 Locate and remove the screws holding the drive inside the 5-inch bay. There are normally four screws mounted at the side of the drive.

6 Slide the drive out through either the front or back of the bay, insert the replacement drive and affix screws to secure the new drive in the bay.

7 Insert the data and power cables into the back of the new drive. Make sure that both the notch and the red line are as they were on the original drive.

8 Place the lid back on the case and fix the screws back in place. Reconnect the power cable.

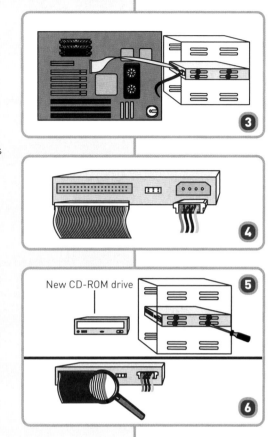

New CD-ROM drive

New Hardware Found **9**

CD Rom Device

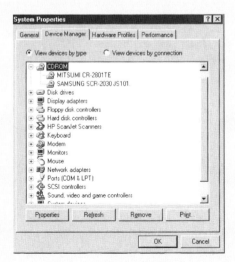

9 Restart the system. Windows should now detect the new device and request a driver disk. With this floppy disk Windows can install the necessary software to control the CD-ROM. Your new CD-ROM drive will appear when you double-click on the '**My Computer**' icon.

What to do if the new drive does not work

Go back to step 7 and make sure the cables are securely connected, the right way round. Try the ribbon cable the other way (if it will fit). The drive will not be damaged if the data cable is placed the wrong way round. Make sure that the device is displayed under '**System Properties**'.

How CD-ROMs work

The principle behind the working of a CD-ROM is quite simple. The surface of each disk has tiny reflective mirrors. The mirrors are arranged at an angle so that when a laser from the playing head strikes the mirrors, light is bounced to sensors on the left or the right. Each of these sensors represents a one or a zero, so the information can be represented in binary code.

REPLACING A FLOPPY-DISK DRIVE

Before you start

Check your PC warranty. Although the task itself is relatively easy, there may be aspects of the design of your PC that affect the way an upgrade must be carried out. Most PC vendors provide experts on a technical support phone line to advise on such matters. If you are unsure, consult these experts before you begin.

Warning!

The main source of danger when working inside a PC is electricity. To protect yourself and your PC, take the following steps (see also page 133).

- Ensure the PC is still plugged in to the mains power but the wall socket is turned off.

- Touch the fingers of both hands on a metal part of the PC chassis to remove static electricity from your body before touching any components.

Like any electronic device, a floppy-disk drive has a finite life span. This section shows how to test the drive on your PC and carry out simple repairs. If the drive is beyond repair, you need to replace it. Follow the manufacturer's instructions in the context of this section's advice.

The 3½-inch-floppy-disk drive is found in most desktop PCs. If you believe that the drive on your PC has stopped working, try the following:

- use a disk from another computer
- make sure that the write-protect tab (on the top right-hand corner) is correctly positioned. You can save files on to the disk only if this tab is in the closed position. The tab protects files from accidental deletion
- buy a fresh set of blank 3½-inch disks and try formatting them
- copy files using DOS (see section 5.8)
- make sure your anti-virus software is up to date
- make sure that the floppy disk is listed in the POST screen when the PC first starts up.

If after all these tests you find you need to replace the drive, you will need a new floppy-disk drive. These cost £15–£20.

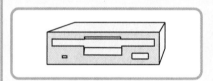

How to install a floppy-disk drive

1 In Windows, go to the **'System Information'** (see section 1.10) screen and remove the old floppy-disk device. Then power the system down.

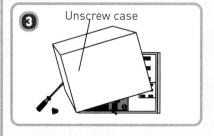

Switch off from the mains

Anti-static protector

2 Turn the power off at the mains and take anti-static precautions (see margin).

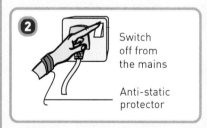

Unscrew case

3 Open the chassis, locate the cables which run from the computer's motherboard and power-supply unit to the rear of the floppy-disk drive. Remove the larger ribbon-style data cable from the back of the floppy disk drive, taking note of which way up it fitted into the drive. To help you, most cables have a red line down one side and a notch on the top of the plastic connector.

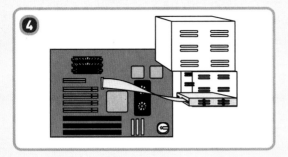

4 Trace the second, smaller cable which runs from the floppy disk drive to the power supply. This power cable fits in only one way. Remove this cable from the back of the drive.

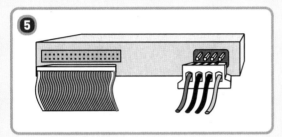

5 Locate and remove the screws holding the floppy disk drive inside the 3½-inch bay. There are normally four screws mounted at the side of the drive.

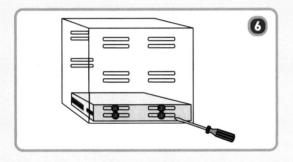

6 Slide the drive out through either the front or back of the bay, insert the replacement drive and affix screws to secure the new drive in the bay.

How floppy disks work

A floppy-disk drive works on a similar principle to a record-player but uses magnetic properties instead of grooves and pits. A magnetic sensor (read head) moves over the surface of the disk looking for patterns of positively charged areas to determine stored information. The opposite happens when storing information - a small magnet (write head) changes the magnetic field on parts of the disk depending on the information it needs to save.

7 Insert the floppy drive data cable into the back of the new drive. Make sure that both the notch and the red line are as they were when the original drive was installed. Insert the power cable, taking care not to force either cable.

8 Place the lid back on the case and fix the screws back in place. Reconnect the power cable and test your new floppy disk drive.

What to do if the new drive does not work

If the floppy drive activity light is permanently on or no light comes on when you try to access the drive, go back to step 7 and make sure the data cable is connected the right way round and securely attached. Try the cable the other way (if it will fit). The drive will not be damaged if the data cable is placed the wrong way round.

Go into the PC's BIOS (see section 5.2) and make sure that the 3½-inch floppy disk drive is listed and is set to the 1.44Mb mode.

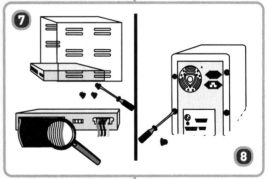

Warning!

Make sure that no foreign objects, such as coins, have been forced into the drive slot by inexperienced users or children, or that the shutter has not come off a disk and stayed inside. This can stop the floppy-disk drive from working.

UPGRADING YOUR SOUND SYSTEM

Before you start

Before you start to upgrade your soundcard, consult the terms of your PC warranty. There may be aspects of the design of your PC that affect the way an upgrade must be carried out. Most PC vendors provide experts on a technical support phone line to advise on such matters. If you are unsure, consult them before you begin.

Warning!

The main source of danger when working inside a PC is electricity. To protect yourself and your PC, take the following steps (see also page 133).

- Ensure the PC is still plugged in to the mains power but the wall socket is turned off.

- Touch the fingers of both hands on a metal part of the PC chassis to remove static electricity from your body before touching any components.

The soundcard is an incredibly reliable part of the PC system. If you are a keen musician, you may want to upgrade the soundcard to one more suited to your creative endeavour. Although this is a relatively simple task, integrating the new card into a complete multimedia system is more complex. Follow the manufacturer's instructions in the context of this section's advice.

Many PCs now come with a built-in soundcard. Budget soundcards, although adequate for multimedia, are of limited use for musicians. On lower-cost or business-orientated PCs, many manufacturers embed the sound features directly on to the motherboard. This makes the PC simpler to manufacture and set up, but hinders upgrading.

Before upgrading your soundcard, find out what type of card best suits your needs and the constraints of your PC. Some soundcards offer features such as extra memory for holding extended MIDI samples or a port able to accept digital input from other audio devices. You also need to identify physically what type of slots are available for your soundcard upgrade.

Using the Windows 'Properties' screen (see section 1.10) you can find many details about your sound system before opening the chassis. The main features to look for are the amount of RAM available for MIDI and the make and model of the existing soundcard. This information can help you decide which type of soundcard to upgrade to. Having extra MIDI RAM memory is useful for musicians. Comparing the make and model with others from the same supplier helps to ascertain which features will be available after upgrading to a newer model.

To make sure that the new soundcard is suitable for your PC, open the chassis and locate your existing sound system by tracing the speaker socket to either a plug-in card or the motherboard. If the sound sub-system is on the motherboard it is very unlikely that this can be upgraded. If the sound system is on a card, you need to find out if it uses an ISA or PCI slot (the former is much longer than the latter). The diagram on page 146 should help.

If you have decided to upgrade your soundcard and the existing card is built in to the PC's motherboard, you must disable it before your new sound hardware will work correctly. To do this you need to do two things:

- remove the device from your 'System Properties' (see section 1.10)
- enter the BIOS (see section 5.2) and disable the soundcard located under the 'Sound, Video and Game Controllers' section of the 'System Properties'.

How to upgrade your soundcard

1 When you have bought a new soundcard and are ready to install it, first go into 'System Properties' (see section 1.10) in Windows and remove the existing sound driver. Then power the system down.

2 Turn the power off at the mains and take anti-static precautions (see opposite margin).

3 Open the chassis and remove the existing soundcard. A single screw normally holds this in place.

4 Insert the new card into an appropriate slot, making sure it is firmly seated. If it will not slide in smoothly, check that the card matches the slot. Once it is inserted, screw the card into place and secure the chassis.

5 Reconnect all the cables including those to the speakers and restart your PC. Windows should now detect a new soundcard and ask for the driver disk supplied by the soundcard manufacturer. The system may need to restart after this but once restarted should work with the new soundcard.

What to do if the new soundcard does not work

If you turn the computer back on after installing the new card and the soundcard does not work:

- open the case and make sure that the card is seated securely
- make sure that the speaker cable is also securely fastened to the new soundcard output port
- if you have a soundcard built on to the motherboard, try your speakers in the old speaker sockets. Play a sound on your PC: if the old sound system is still active, you need to enter the BIOS (see section 5.2) and disable the onboard sound
- have a look at the section on sound troubleshooting (section 4.9).

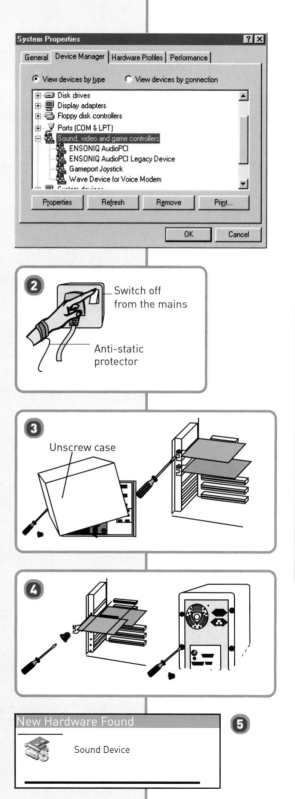

UPGRADING YOUR MODEM

Before you start

Before you start to upgrade your modem, consult the terms of your PC warranty. There may be aspects of the design of your PC that affect the way an upgrade must be carried out. Most PC vendors provide experts on a technical support phone line to advise on such matters. If you are unsure, consult them before you begin.

Warning!

The main source of danger when working inside a PC is electricity. To protect yourself and your PC, take the following steps (see also page 133).

- Ensure the PC is still plugged in to the mains power but the wall socket is turned off.

- Touch the fingers of both hands on a metal part of the PC chassis to remove static electricity from your body before touching any components.

A modem is a device (connected using a telephone line) used to surf the Internet, access emails and send and receive faxes. It may be external or internal. Upgrading an external modem simply involves buying a new one and plugging it in; upgrading an internal one is more complex. This section covers the most common method of doing so. Follow the manufacturer's instructions in the context of this section's advice.

Many PCs now come with a built-in modem, which hinders upgrading. Find out what type of modem will best suit your needs and the constraints of your PC. Some modems offer extra features such as a built-in answerphone which works independently of the PC.

Using the Windows **'Properties'** screen (see section 1.10) you can find many details about your modem before opening the chassis. The main feature to look for is the 'standard' the modem uses - it is called the 'V' standard or is referred to in terms of speed, e.g. 56k or 33.6k. This information can help you decide which type of modem to upgrade to. Some modems plug directly into the serial ports of your PC and are the easiest to upgrade. At the moment the fastest speed for modems using a normal telephone line is 56k.

To make sure that the new modem is suitable for your PC, open the chassis and locate your existing modem by tracing the telephone cable slot to either a plug-in card or the motherboard. If the modem is on the motherboard it is very unlikely that this can be upgraded. If the modem is on a card, you need to find out if it uses an ISA or PCI slot (the former is much longer than the latter). The diagram below should help.

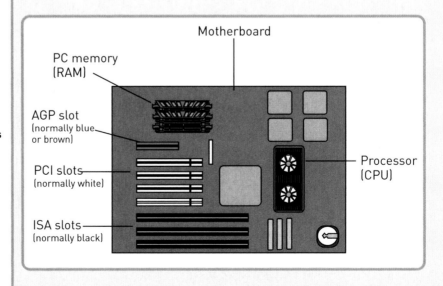

How to upgrade your modem

1 When you have bought a new modem and are ready to install it, first go into '**System Properties**' (see section 1.10) in Windows and remove the existing modem. Then power down the system.

2 Turn off the power at the mains and take anti-static precautions (see opposite margin).

3 Open the chassis and remove the existing modem card. A single screw normally holds this in place.

4 Insert the new card into the previously occupied slot, making sure it is firmly seated. If it will not slide in smoothly, check that the card matches the slot. Once it is inserted, screw the card into place and secure the chassis.

5 Reconnect all the cables and restart your PC. Windows should now detect a new modem and ask for the driver disk supplied by the modem manufacturer. The system may need to restart after this, but once restarted should work with the new modem.

6 Any application that uses the modem may need to have its settings changed to point to the new modem.

What to do if the new modem does not work

If you turn the computer back on after installing the new card and the modem does not work:

- open the case and make sure that the card is seated securely
- make sure that the telephone cable is in the correct slot. If your modem has two sockets for a telephone jack, try making a telephone call with an attached handset. If you cannot, switch the cables round
- if you have a modem built on to the motherboard, try the telephone lead in this slot instead. If it still works you need to enter the BIOS (see section 5.2) and disable the onboard modem
- look at the sections on modem or Internet troubleshooting (sections 5.7 and 7.6).

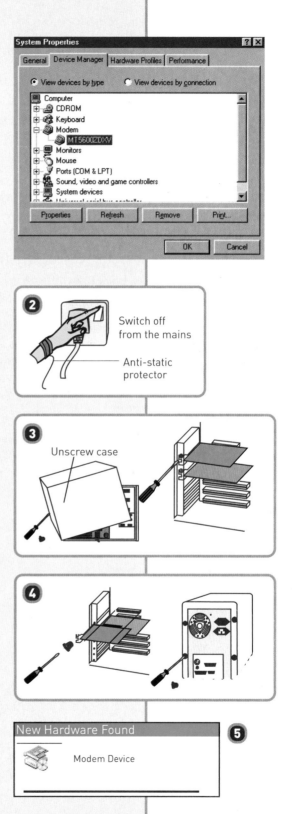

Switch off from the mains

Anti-static protector

Unscrew case

New Hardware Found

Modem Device

REPLACING A HARD-DISK DRIVE (II)

Before you start

Replacing a hard disk is a complex job because many of the pre-installed applications and settings may be available only from the original PC manufacturer. Before you start to replace the hard disk, consult the terms of your PC warranty.

Warning!

The main source of danger when working inside a PC is electricity. To protect yourself and your PC, take the following steps (see also page 133).

- Ensure the PC is still plugged in to the mains power but the wall socket is turned off.

- Touch the fingers of both hands on a metal part of the PC chassis to remove static electricity from your body before touching any components.

Hard-disk drives are mechanical, not electronic, devices and eventually wear out through use. Although the death of a hard drive does not mean you need a new PC, replacing the drive is a complex task. Follow the manufacturer's instructions in the context of the advice in this section and the next.

If you have a consistent backup strategy (see section 2.4), the failure of a hard disk is an annoyance but not a major worry. Generally, hard disks die gradually. You will first notice that files become corrupt, then, as this gets worse, one day the drive will simply refuse to start up. Note that if you turn on your machine and the system fails to start, it may not be indicative of a dead hard disk. It may be that a critical file is damaged and needs replacing. So before throwing away a perfectly fixable hard disk, run the following tests:

- try using a boot disk (see section 2.4) to access the drive via DOS. If the drive is functioning correctly it may mean that Windows needs to be fixed (see section 5.9) and that a new drive is not needed
- try running ScanDisk (see section 2.2) from within Windows or DOS. ScanDisk can provide a temporary fix for a dying disk
- make sure that no floppy disks (or CD-ROMS) are in the PC at boot-up
- if you have anti-virus software, try running it from a clean boot disk. Some of the nastier viruses can prevent a PC from starting up correctly
- check the PC's BIOS (see section 5.2) and make sure that the hard disk is listed correctly. After a sudden power cut, the PC can 'forget' the vital statistics of a drive
- open the case and make sure that the power and data cables have not been detached from the hard disk.

If after all these tests you find you need to replace the drive, you will need:

- a new internal hard-disk drive. These cost between £80 and £160 and are

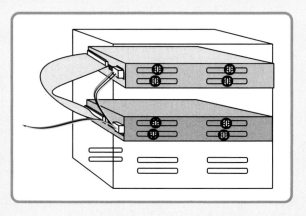

available from most computer stores. The majority of desktop PCs use IDE drives, but some powerful systems use SCSI disks (see Glossary)˙

- Windows 98 software including DOS boot disk (not an upgrade copy)
- DOS CD-ROM drivers on 3$\frac{1}{2}$-inch floppy disks (available on request from the manufacturer).

If your hard disk can be coaxed to work, make a copy of all your important documents on floppy disks or Zip cartridges as fast as you can – the new hard disk will be empty.

How to replace a hard-disk drive

1 Turn the power off at the mains and take anti-static precautions (see margin).

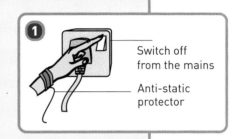

Switch off from the mains

Anti-static protector

2 Open the chassis, locate and remove the existing hard disk, and place the new hard disk in the same drive mount. Make sure that both the power and data cables are as they were when the old drive was in place.

3 Some computer systems allow you to boot up straight from a CD-ROM disk. To test if yours can, place your Windows 98 CD-ROM in the drive and power the system up. If the Windows set-up program runs, follow the on-screen instructions. If, after you insert the Windows 98 installation CD, the system fails to perform the set-up procedure, you will have to set up the disk manually. See next section.

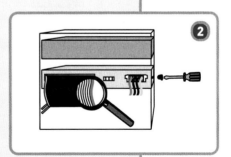

4 If Windows does install automatically, you may find that it asks you to install various device drivers for items such as the soundcard, modem and printer. These are normally provided with the PC on either floppy disks or CD. If you do not have these disks, contact your PC manufacturer.

What to do if the new drive does not work

You may not have a bootable CD-ROM drive (see point 3 above). Make sure that the settings in the BIOS (see section 5.2) are set for booting first from a CD-ROM. Make sure all cables are securely fitted and are the right way round.

REPLACING A HARD-DISK DRIVE (II)

Partitioning disks

If you have a particularly large hard-disk drive, setting up multiple partitions is useful for organising the files and applications on your PC.

You can use one partition for the Windows system, one for applications and another for data files. This means you can back up just your valuable data files without wasting backup capacity on applications which you already have on CD-ROM.

This section is to be read after the previous one. If your PC cannot boot up from a CD-ROM, you need to follow the instructions in this section to complete the installation of your hard disk. Again, follow the manufacturer's instructions in the context of this section's advice.

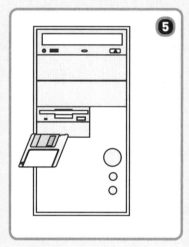

How to replace a hard-disk drive (continued)

5 If your PC is not capable of booting up from a CD-ROM, you need to initialise the new hard-disk drive using a bootable floppy disk. (For information on making a bootable floppy disk see section 2.4). Turn the PC off, place the boot disk in the floppy disk drive and turn the PC on again.

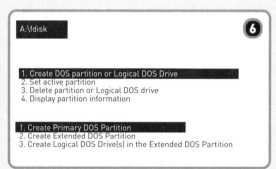

```
A:\fdisk                                          6

1. Create DOS partition or Logical DOS Drive
2. Set active partition
3. Delete partition or Logical DOS drive
4. Display partition information


1. Create Primary DOS Partition
2. Create Extended DOS Partition
3. Create Logical DOS Drive(s) in the Extended DOS Partition
```

6 After the PC has booted up from the floppy disk, A:\ appears on the screen. At this point you need to partition and format the disk. To set a partition, type 'FDISK' and follow the on-screen instructions to create a single DOS partition. From this screen you can set up more than one virtual drive on each disk. These partitions each have a unique letter identifying them. However, the main partition (or boot partition) must be the C: drive.

7 Next, format the disk to allow Windows to be installed. You need to type 'FORMAT C: /S' and follow the on-screen prompts. You will need to format extra partitions separately for Windows to recognise them. To do this, type in 'FORMAT' (partition letter): but you do not need to type the '/S' syntax, which copies the system files on to the drive. Next, reboot your PC – the system should now boot up without the aid of a floppy disk, and end up with a C:\ prompt on the screen.

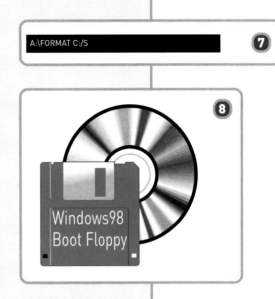

```
A:\FORMAT C:/S                                    7
```

8 With your Windows CD you should have received a Windows boot floppy. Place this disk in the floppy drive and the Windows 98 CD in the CD-ROM drive and reboot the system. If the Windows set-up program begins, move on to step 10, otherwise follow step 9.

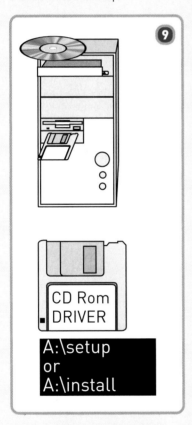

9 If you do not have a Windows installation floppy disk, you need to install your DOS CD-ROM drivers to allow your CD-ROM drive to function before you can install Windows. The driver diskette will normally have a SETUP.EXE or INSTALL.EXE program to automate this procedure. If you do not have a CD-ROM driver disk, contact your PC manufacturer or look on the web site of the manufacturer of your CD-ROM. Once your CD-ROM drive is working in DOS, switch to the CD-ROM (usually D:) and type 'SETUP'. This will launch the Windows 98 set-up program. Follow the on-screen instructions.

10 After Windows has started, re-store your old system files using the backup method of your choice. You may find that some applications will not work from the backup, so you may have to re-install them. Many of your system settings will also have changed.

What to do if the new drive does not work

If your drive does not work, test that all the cables are securely attached and that the BIOS (see section 5.2) has correctly recognised the new drive.

FAQS ON UPGRADING

Upgrading a PC can give rise to queries and problems. Here are some of the most commonly asked questions and some possible solutions.

If I upgrade my PC, will it invalidate my warranty?
In 99 per cent of cases, no. However, occasionally some companies that sell PCs insist that any upgrades are carried out with them because the machine contains non-standard parts (or because it was sold to you under a special deal). If this is the case, you should have been informed of it when you bought your PC.

What can I do with my old parts after an upgrade?
Many companies will buy second-hand computer equipment. The prices range from a third to half the price the dealer thinks he can sell the item for.

Is buying upgrades via mail order a good idea?
You can save a great deal of money by buying hardware direct, via mail order. However, if your upgrade is not suitable, faulty or incompatible, you will have to pay the cost of delivery yourself, unless you can prove that the company was at fault.

The company which sold me my PC has gone bust. Where can I get repairs?
Most PCs use standard components that are widely available from any PC repair or service company. If you need a repair or upgrade, quote the make and model of the PC and get confirmation that the company is able to service your machine before you send any cash.

My laptop is faulty. Can I repair it myself?
Laptops use specialised parts that are far more difficult to repair or replace than those of standard PCs. Even opening a laptop without proper training could dislodge sensitive components. Contact the manufacturer for a list of authorised repair centres and use one of them instead.

Can I upgrade my monitor's performance?
Unfortunately not. If you decide to buy a new monitor, keep the older one as a spare as monitors tend to hold their value and are a useful basis for building a second system.

My PC appears to be getting slower the more I use it. Is this possible?

Yes, in a way. The PC is probably performing at the same speed but you may have loaded more applications such as anti-virus programs, electronic address books, colourful wallpaper, screen savers and the like, which all take up a bit of memory. You can download free **'benchtesting'** software to test the performance of your PC, and you can retest your PC's benchmark whenever you want to make sure your machine is not slowing down in any way.

I play a lot of games that run o.k. — but only at low resolution. How can I improve the images?

You need to increase the amount of video RAM to be able to play at screen resolutions greater than 640 x 480. You also need a monitor larger than 14 inches to benefit from increased video RAM.

I've upgraded a device and now another device has stopped working. What shall I do?

This is quite common. Many of the devices in your PC rely on one another. Try removing the affected device from your Windows system settings (see section 1.10), then restart your PC. When your PC starts it will try to join the two devices together so they can communicate again. If this fails, you may need to contact the hardware manufacturer of the new device you have bought.

I've bought an upgrade which uses the USB socket but it doesn't work. What can I do?

USB is a relatively new concept. You need to make sure that you are running at least Windows 98 for USB to work correctly. Also, some older machines had USB sockets but their features may have been turned off in the BIOS (see section 5.2).

I want to upgrade my PC but I've run out of slots to put new devices in. What can I do?

This is a very common problem. The easiest way is to buy external versions of the devices you want to add, e.g. use an external modem or network card instead of the slots inside your machine. If this is not possible, you may be able to buy devices that do more than one job but take up only one slot, e.g. a soundcard with built-in modem or graphics card with a built-in video capture card.

I'm running out of hard disk space for my documents. What can I do?

You have three options. You could buy a second hard disk and fit this into your machine, which requires some technical savvy (see sections 6.8 and 6.9). Another option would be to use a removable device such as a CD writer, tape backup or ZIP disk and move your infrequently used files to removable media: this option is easiest but moving files can be slow and the cost of some types of media quite high. The third option is to use Windows' built-in drive compression software (see section 2.8).

My keyboard [or mouse] is sluggish or temperamental. What can I do?

Keyboards and mice are not as durable as many computer components and are exposed to dirt and grime. Try cleaning your mouse or keyboard with a computer cleaning kit. Even if you do this regularly, expect to have to replace them after a few years.

For many people Internet access, for education, entertainment, communication and e-commerce, is a key reason for owning a PC. The number of new Internet users is growing apace and the desktop PC is the catalyst for this growth. Desktop PCs can also send and receive data by electronic facsimile, bulletin boards or over wide area networks. The humble modem plays a key role in each one of these tasks and as such is vital for anybody wanting to join the information super highway. Not only can the modem connect to the Internet but it can also send and receive facsimiles without the need for paper.

For most home users, the telephone is the simplest and most cost-effective way to communicate with other computers. This may change with the reduction in cost of ISDN lines or even the new high-speed ADSL services currently being developed.

To use any of the data services available via the telephone, you will need a modem. Most modern PCs incorporate a modem, but if yours does not, fitting one is reasonably straightforward (see section 6).

The main problems associated with the Internet are of compatibility and reliability. The Internet, for all its wonders, can still be painfully slow. New standards and applications are starting to appear on an almost daily basis, each with their own benefits and related problems.

Security is also a big concern — not only in the context of buying online but also because so much undesirable, even harmful, content is widely available on the web. Viruses, illegal software and pornography all make the web a place in which to tread with caution. Computer systems and users can be protected from these pitfalls by low-cost or even free software, some of which is built into Windows.

This section explains how to set up your system for the Internet and fix the most common problems that you are likely to encounter.

COMMUNICATION, NETWORKING AND THE INTERNET

7.1 Connecting to the Internet
Different ways to connect to the Internet.

7.2 The Internet browser
Overview of the world's most popular Internet browser.

7.3 Browser options
How to set up common features of Internet Explorer.

7.4 Typical email software
How to send and receive email.

7.5 Downloading software
How to find software on the Internet and how to
download it to your PC.

7.6 Internet troubleshooting
Quick fixes for problems you may encounter with
your Internet connection.

7.7 Fax software
How to set up your PC's fax facilities.

7.8 Introducing newsgroups
How to search for and join newsgroups.

7.9 Creating your own web site
Tips for creating your own web site.

CONNECTING TO THE INTERNET

ISP or online service?

Unless you are a government, a university or a relatively large business, you cannot connect your computers directly to the Internet. Instead, you have to connect to an intermediary.

Two types of company exist to do this. Internet service providers (ISPs offer connection to the Internet for a monthly fee, which is generally low or even free), and offer a no-frills connection to the web.

Online service providers (OSPs) such as AOL and CompuServe are generally more costly but offer substantial proprietary content which can be accessed only by subscribers. This extra content may include built-in parental controls, online games or edutainment software.

However, the boundaries between ISPs and OSPs are blurring more and more as OSPs lower their prices and ISPs try to make themselves stand out by offering more content, sometimes at no charge.

The Internet is now part of everyday life for many PC users. A huge number of companies offers Internet connections and services. This section explains how the Internet works and what types of connection are available.

Getting online

Every Internet service provider offers you a CD-ROM to help you connect to the Internet. This CD-ROM contains all the settings and software, such as browsers, you need to sign up. You simply follow the instructions that come with the CD-ROM and within 10 minutes you can be online.

Many services are free. They normally include a number of email addresses that you can create and some space for hosting your own home web page. Often the difference between a free service and a paid-for service is the number of extra features your ISP offers. These include multiple access points around the world — so, if you are abroad, you can retrieve your email by dialling a local number; free online games; reference material; and better technical support on Internet matters.

Also, free providers are unlikely to support faster-connection technologies such as ISDN, cable modems or DSL.

Modem If you connect to the Internet from home, your computer probably uses a modem. The word derives from modulator-demodulator, and the device translates computer information into a form which can be transmitted over an ordinary telephone line.

Most current modems conform to the V.90 standard established by the International Telecommunications Union, which you should look for in the specifications of any modem you are considering. This ensures that the modem is theoretically capable of downloading information at 56 kilobits per second, which equates to 1Mb in about 2 minutes.

In real life the connection speed depends on the quality of your telephone line (between 40 and 48kbits/sec is common), but this is fast enough for you to read most web pages fairly quickly.

ISDN Effectively a digital telephone line, ISDN (Integrated Services Digital Network) offers you a minimum connection speed of 64kbits/sec to your ISP. However, because all ISDN installations include at least two lines (known as channels) you can combine these to give an effective access speed of 128kbits/sec or even more.

The installation cost of ISDN is high, and if you want speeds above 64kbits/sec you will be charged for making two or more access calls simultaneously. However, the connection time for each call is much quicker on a digital line (typically five seconds, compared to 45 or so using a modem), and as long as you have a free channel you can make voice calls even while you are on the Web.

GSM and WAP (mobile phones) It is possible to connect to the Internet using a digital mobile phone: all those sold in the UK currently use the GSM standard. However, the speed of connection is very slow (less than a fifth of the speed of a normal phone line) so Web-surfing is extremely tedious. New mobile technologies will soon make connections faster, but in the meantime it is best to reserve GSM connections for quickly checking your email.

To connect via a mobile phone, you need a phone handset which can make data as well as voice calls. Some include a GSM modem: if yours does not, you will also need a modem card which can connect to your phone.

ADSL (broadband) ADSL (asynchronous digital subscriber line) allows your computer to be connected to the Internet permanently. Although it uses the same wires as your phone line, you do not incur any extra charges for the time that you are online and you can make voice calls at the same time.

At the time of writing, only trial services are available, but BT has announced its OpenWorld service. Using this, ADSL will offer speeds of 512kbits/sec (a maximum of 2Mbit/sec is theoretically possible) and cost £50–£100 a month all-inclusive.

Cable modem Cable modems are a curious hybrid technology. As the name suggests, they are used by cable TV companies to offer Internet access using the same fibre-optic cables that bring television pictures into your home.

No services are yet available in the UK but the US experience suggests that you will have to sign up with the ISP arm of the cable company: pricing is likely to be related to any package of other services you subscribe to. Speeds are comparable to or even greater than ADSL and you can still use your phone while you surf the Net.

LAN (local area network) You are most likely to encounter a LAN at work. It is used to connect several computers together, allowing their users to share files with each other and access common resources such as printers and scanners. However, the LAN may also be connected to the Internet. In this case, it allows all the attached computers to access the Net as well. As the LAN is likely to be connected to an expensive but speedy leased line or using several ISDN channels, Internet access using it will be rapid.

The Web is the Internet

The Internet is the generic term for the worldwide network of interlinked computers to which you connect whenever you dial into your ISP. Conceived in 1969, as the American military's ARPAnet, a system for the exchange of scientific information, it was joined by other organisations, mainly universities and research agencies, in the 1970s and 80s. Thereafter, it became publicly accessible.

The Web, a comparatively recent development, is the most accessible part of the Internet. It uses protocols developed at the CERN research labs (and credited to the Englishman Tim Berners-Lee) to make the information stored on the Net accessible using graphical browsers.

Usenet, better known as Newsgroups, is a further subset of the Internet: it allows fast text-only discussion forums to thrive. And the most common application of all, email, relies on Internet-connected computers to transmit messages.

THE INTERNET BROWSER

What's in a name?

Traditionally, the suffix at the end of a web address indicated the type of organisation to which it belonged. The .com suffix stands for a commercial body whereas .org usually means an American or international institution such as a special-interest group, charity, government agency or educational institution. Other countries use suffixes such as .co.uk (commercial, UK) or .gov.fr (government, France). However, these conventions are not always adhered to. The .uk suffix indicates a UK-friendly address, but may in fact be hosted overseas.

The most common Internet browser is Microsoft's Internet Explorer. This piece of software allows you to connect to the Internet, view web sites and download content. This section explains the basics of the browser interface.

1 Menu options

2 Go to previous page

3 If you have already gone back a page, this will take you forward a page

4 'Stop' aborts the loading of the current page

5 If a page is not displaying correctly, 'Refresh' will attempt to load the page again

6 Clicking on 'Home' will launch the default start page for your browser. This can be changed via the options described in the next section

7 'Search' will launch the default search tools for finding items on the Internet

8 Internet site address

9 Each bit of underlined text on this web page is a link to another page. Most

web sites use either an underline or text of a different colour to highlight a link you can click on for instant connection. Clicking on it takes you to the linked item, which may be a page on the same site or one on a different site

10 This bar provides information on what the browser is

currently doing. If you leave the mouse over a link, it will also give you some information on where that link will take you

11 This bar is a graphical representation of how complete the loading of a page is. Eventually, when all the items on the page are loaded, the bar disappears

12 Calls up a list of your favourite sites. To add (or 'bookmark') sites click on '**Favorites**' on the top toolbar

13 '**History**' stores a list of web sites you have been to over the last few weeks

14 The '**Channels**' button calls up a list of news, entertainment and shopping web sites. This list has several entries by default but can be added to in a similar way to your favourites

15 Clicking on '**Fullscreen**' toggles the browser between the standard view and a special mode that hides a lot of the menus and buttons. Moving the mouse to the top of the screen brings back some of the options and allows you to toggle back to the standard mode

16 Clicking on '**Mail**' launches the default mail program

17 Clicking on '**Print**' triggers the printing of the current web page

18 If you have compatible web publishing software, the '**Edit**' icon may appear. This allows you to grab the page for editing

19 Many web sites have a search facility on them. In this example, typing a word and clicking on '**Go**' starts a search of the entire BBC web site for instances of the word typed. When a match is found, another click will take you to the relevant page.

Speed tip

By right-clicking on a picture on a web site then selecting 'Save As', you can store images from the web on your PC. However, if you decide to republish any of these images you must first obtain permission from the web site's owner.

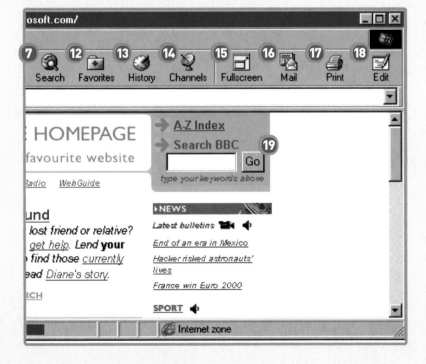

Warning!

When buying goods over the Internet, try to use your own credit card. Most credit card companies now offer protection schemes for goods bought over the Net and which include insurance against fraud. Contact your credit card company for more details.

7 | Communication, networking and the Internet

BROWSER OPTIONS

Other types of browsers

The biggest rival to Microsoft's browser dominance is Netscape Communicator. Netscape created one of the first widely used browsers and has a loyal following. However, Microsoft's insistence that its rival Internet Explorer browser be included in the Windows Operating System gave rise to both legal action and the reduction of Netscape's market leadership. Netscape Communicator is still free and available from www.netscape.com.

For users of services such as AOL, the browser is a special version only for use with that service. These browsers normally come with extensive help files and additional features such as parental protection, electronic banking software or built-in online chat software. However, these services may cost extra.

Configuring your browser for general operation and managing security is essential for safe and happy web surfing.

The main Internet Explorer options can be found under Tools/Internet Options from the main menu bar.

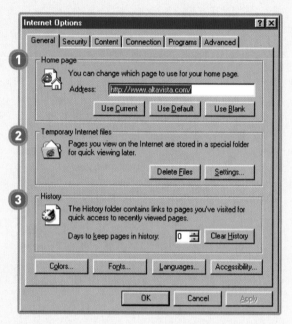

1 You can change your home page via this option. This is the page that the software loads up first, each time you connect to the Internet

2 Temporary files can take up quite a bit of hard disk space but improve the loading speed of frequently used web sites. By clicking on settings, you can alter how much hard disk space is used for temporary files. The '**Delete Files**' option removes temporary files, freeing up hard disk space

3 By increasing the number of days kept in the history file, you can find web pages you visited some time ago by clicking on the '**History**' button within your browser. For security or privacy you may, however, want to keep your history and temporary file folder short.

The four options along the bottom, **Colors**, **Fonts**, **Languages** and **Accessibility**, control how Internet Explorer and web pages are displayed. For the most part these options are rarely touched. However, they are quite self-explanatory, allowing you to change default colours, fonts and preferred languages. The accessibility options are designed to improve legibility for partially sighted users.

Internet Explorer has a number of pre-set security options, arranged under a scheme called '**zones**'. However, for home users the Internet is treated as a single zone called the '**Internet zone**'. Zones are used in a business environment and you have a different security model depending whether you are connecting to a web site hosted within your company or an external one.

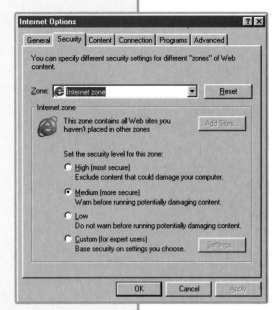

The different default security settings range from low to high. On the lowest setting, many types of Internet content such as web-based applications and documents are automatically loaded and executed. Also, details about your computer and your user information are transmitted without warning across the Internet. On the highest setting, every time non-standard content is about to be downloaded, the browser will give you the option of refusing it. Also, information about you is withheld or confirmation is required before this information is sent across the Internet.

For the majority of users, the medium settings are a good balance. Expert users can set up their own security preferences by selecting the custom option. Within this are several options for restricting type of content. For more information on these content types, consult the built-in help file by pressing F1 while on the 'custom' settings page.

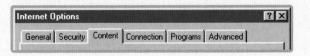

The other options within Internet Explorer are **Content**, **Connection**, **Programs** and **Advanced**.

Content contains information about you and tools for screening out undesirable sites. Unfortunately, the built-in content-screening software is not effective as the system has only a tiny number of sites which have been rated. Third-party products can be bought to protect children from viewing explicit web sites (see section 3.11). Although these cost extra, they are far superior to the built-in protection software.

Connection is useful only if you have more than one connection to the Internet. From here, you can select which connection to establish. For example, if you have a Freeserve and a Demon account, you can select which one to access via this option.

Programs lists the default programs that will be launched if you click on the email or news icons within your browser.

Advanced lists over 40 options for tweaking your browser. Pressing F1 on this screen gives you more information on the tweaks you can make to the operation of your browser.

Upgrade to heaven

Newer versions of popular Internet browsers are constantly becoming available. Before you upgrade, write down the settings you need to set up your connection manually, in case the automatic upgrade procedure fails. This information is found under the Connection tab. Don't change anything, but instead write down your login details, password, connection types, access telephone number and any other pertinent information.

The current version of Internet Explorer is version 5.0. However, the most popular is the 4.x series.

TYPICAL EMAIL SOFTWARE

There are many email programs, of which Microsoft Outlook Express is one of the most popular. From within this package you can send and receive emails as well as managing your contact details.

1 Compose a new email message

2 Reply to a message in your Inbox

3 Reply to a message which has been sent to you as part of a group. With this command you can reply to everyone on the same distribution list

4 Forward a message to another email address

5 **'Send and Receive'** attempts to connect to your ISP, send any email waiting in the Outbox and collect any email waiting for you at your ISP

6 'Delete' removes the email from your Inbox and deletes it

7 These are the emails currently residing within this folder (in this case, your Inbox)

8 List of possible folders where emails can reside. By right-clicking on the **'Outlook Express'** icon and selecting **'New Folder'** you can create your own filing system for emails

9 You can store details of people you email within the **'Address Book'**. If you receive an email, double-click on it to enlarge it. If you want to add the sender details to your address

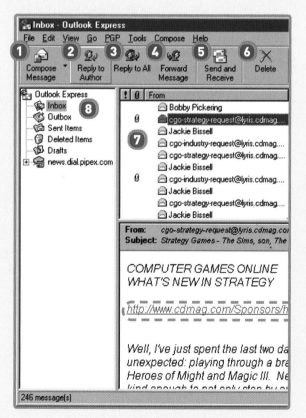

book, select the Tools menu and select 'Add to Address Book'. You are then presented with a form so that, if you wish, you can add extra details such as telephone number and postal address

10 The header tool bar allows you to organise your mailbox quickly, either by sender's name (from), the email's subject, the

date received or according to how the sender has described you. Click on the heading to sort by that column. Click on the heading again to sort the other way round (e.g. most recent first/oldest first)

11 Clicking on a link within an email launches your web browser and loads the indicated page

12 This box shows a preview of the email message that has been selected. Double-clicking on an email will expand the view to full size.

Are you getting attached?

As well as containing text, emails can also have files attached to them. Emails with an attached file normally have a paper clip displayed to the left of the message (see email listing opposite). To save an attachment from an email on to your PC, open the email by double-clicking on it, then select 'File', then select 'Save all attachments'. The computer prompts you for a location in which to save the attached documents and the files are transferred to your PC.

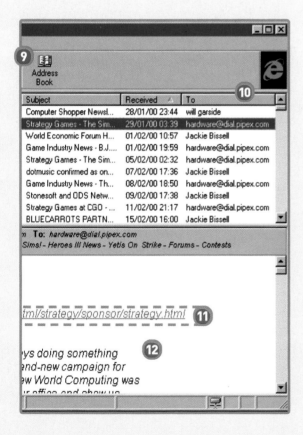

DOWNLOADING SOFTWARE

Downloading times

With a standard 56K modem connected to a fast web site, downloading can be a slow process. A good rule of thumb is to allow 5 minutes for every 1Mb of data being downloaded. Heavy traffic on some web sites may reduce the speed of downloading. To help users, some of the bigger sites offer alternative web sites (called mirrors), which are located in different countries. A mirror site for a download with a .uk suffix may provide a much faster download than a US-based web site.

If downloading is very slow, it may be worth connecting at a different time of day, when there is less congestion.

The Internet offers tens of thousands of applications, music tracks, pictures and documents for download on to your computer system. These can normally be found by typing the word **'shareware'** or **'download'** into any Internet search engine such as yahoo.com, altavista.com or hotbot.com. As well as demos of commercial software, you will find a host of free packages to download.

In this example, we are downloading a game from the world's largest online collection of free software at shareware.com.

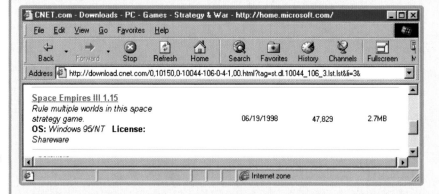

This web site has thousands of programs available for download. They include education, financial software, games and utilities. Next to each entry are listed the date when the software was made available for download, the number of people who have downloaded it and the size of the file measured in megabytes. Clicking on the file name (e.g. Space Empires III) starts the download.

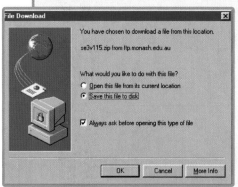

Before the file begins to download from the Internet, the browser asks you whether you wish to save this file to the hard-disk drive on your computer. It also gives you the option to specify the location to which the file is to be downloaded. Files such as documents can be opened directly from the web site using the **'Open this file from its current location'** option. However, this is not an option for very large files (anything over a few kilobytes).

As the file downloads, you receive a constant status report as to the speed of the download and how much of the file has been downloaded.

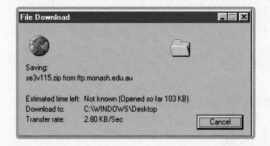

When the file has downloaded, you will receive confirmation of this and a new icon appears in the folder to which you chose to save the file. More often than not, the file is stored in a special compressed format called a Zip file: making the files smaller speeds up downloading from the Internet and makes it possible to store many files inside just one file. To uncompress this file, you need a special utility which can be downloaded from the Internet. The most common of these utilities, called WinZip, is available from web sites which offer shareware or from disks issued free on computer magazine covers.

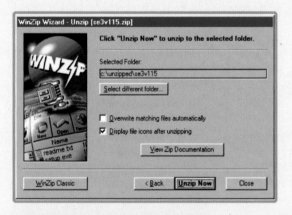

Once you have installed your WinZip program, clicking on the file begins the uncompressing procedure. You will have to specify where you want the file or files to be saved to.

After the unzipping procedure is finished, you are left with a new folder containing your downloaded file or new software. The software normally has a Readme, Setup or Install document with instructions on installation and requirements for using the software.

This is the most common method of downloading files from the Internet. Some sites use different methods but these usually have online help files to explain the differences.

Shareware *vs* freeware

Shareware programs are often complete software applications that the authors have decided to make available for evaluation purposes in the hope that users who like the software will buy it at a future date. Although shareware is free, technical assistance and/or upgrades may be available only to users who have paid.

Freeware, on the other hand, consists of full programs, created by the authors for altruistic reasons. As such, no payment is expected.

Some freeware, such as RealPlayer, QuickTime and browsers like Internet Explorer and Netscape Navigator, are offered free with constant improvements and good technical support. The authors of freeware make money from other packages that complement the free products or through selling advertising or mailing lists generated from the free user base.

It is illegal to resell either shareware or freeware without the authors' consent.

INTERNET TROUBLESHOOTING

The Internet is evolving very fast. New techniques and applications are introduced almost every day. This section offers tips on how to solve the most common Internet problems, including unreliable connections and problems with email.

INTERNET BROWSER PROBLEMS

When I click on the Internet Explorer icon located on my desktop my connection doesn't automatically start.
Click on the **'Home'** icon and see whether the Internet browser attempts to connect. Or close down your Internet browser and mail program and try again. If this does not work, restart the PC, making sure that if you have a multiple-user profiles set-up you log in with the correct name and password.

The Internet browser connects but the speed of my connection is very slow.
Every time you make a connection to your ISP, your modem tests line conditions during the call setup. If line conditions are poor, the transfer rate is reduced to improve reliability. Bad line conditions can be caused by heavy storms, lots of people making calls within your local area or a badly connected telephone extension box. Try reconnecting several times: you may get a better connection speed. Check the connection speed by clicking on the small green box that appears in the lower right-hand corner of the main desktop when a connection is made. The average for a 56K modem is between 40,000bps (40K) and 48,000bps (48K).

Some web pages fail to display correctly. Instead I get rubbish or error messages about 'scripting'.
You may have your security settings too high. On high settings, some types of command sent from web sites are ignored, forcing the page to **'error'**. If the site is trusted, try using the medium- or low-security settings instead (see section 7.3) and reload the page. Otherwise, try changing the resolution of your monitor (see section 3.2). Some web sites are best viewed at 1,024 by 768 resolution instead of the more common 800 by 600 resolution. Make sure that your display settings allow for as many colours as possible.

I type in my user name and password but the Internet browser fails to connect, giving me an incorrect password or login message instead.
Make sure that the Caps Lock key is not active when you type in the password or login as these are often case-sensitive.

If you get your password wrong too many times, some computer systems lock you out for a while. This is to prevent hackers trying common passwords gaining entry to your ISP account. Wait 30 minutes and try again.

I get a connection to the Internet but this drops unexpectedly after a few minutes of use.
If you have other devices on the same phone line, e.g. answerphone or fax, try disconnecting them to see whether this improves reliability.

Look at the connection settings located under (Tools/Internet Options/Connections/Settings) via your browser's menu. The box saying **'Disconnect if idle for XX minutes'** should not be set for less than 5.

Otherwise, contact your ISP for help.

EMAIL PROBLEMS

I am trying to send email to a friend but the mail never reaches the receiver. Instead I get either an error message or no indication of what went wrong.

If you are sending mail with a large attachment, it may have been blocked by the ISP because the attached file is too large. Try sending an email without an attachment to test this possibility.

Some ISPs block emails containing expletives or sexual terms. Check your ISP's policy on email content via its web site or customer support service.

If using an address supplied by the address book, try typing in the email address manually as the address book may be corrupt or contain an incorrect entry.

I want to check my home emails when I'm at work. Is this possible?

Yes. Most ISPs offer web-based tools for checking your email remotely. You will need your login name and password, available from your ISP, to access these.

I keep receiving junk email. Can I block this type of email?

Unfortunately, no. Some ISPs can provide filtering tools to allow you to block emails that come from a certain Internet address but this is not a standard feature provided by all ISPs.

I have received an email with an attachment that I cannot open.

Attached files from emails need a compatible application to be located on your system before it can read them. Make sure that the file is compatible with one of your applications, but instead of double-clicking on the attachment save it to your hard disk first using the **'Save Attachments'** option available from the File menu of most email programs. Next, open the compatible application and load the file into it manually.

Email can be sent from many different types of computers including Apple Macintosh computers, UNIX-based systems and even hand-held computers. Some attachment types may not be compatible with PC architecture and therefore need to be converted before they can be used on a PC. Contact the sender to find out what type of computer and which application program created the attached file.

I've lost an important email among all my messages. How can I find it?

Like many applications, email packages often have a **'Find'** utility. Within Outlook this is located under Edit/Find/Message. By typing in a word under the heading **'Message body'** the software will locate and display any email containing the specified word.

Troubleshooting checklist

• If using an external modem, check whether the modem is plugged into the correct serial port on the computer. There may be more than one of these ports.
• Check whether the phone line is in use by another person or device.

• Check whether your ISP has changed its dial-in number.
• Check whether any fax software is running in the background. If so, turn it off and try again.
• Check that you have logged on under the correct user name.

• Check whether your ISP dial-up number is simply engaged due to heavy traffic.
• Check whether another phone on the same line is off the hook or waiting for a 'ring back' service.

FAX SOFTWARE

If your computer is equipped with a modem you should be able to send and receive faxes, although the software included with Windows is very basic. This section shows you how to send faxes straight from the desktop.

From the start menu, look under Programs/ Accessories/Fax. If no option exists, you need to install it from the Windows CD-ROM. See section 1.8 for how to install Windows utilities.

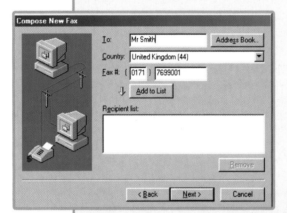

To send a fax, click on the '**Compose new fax**' option. From here you can either pull a fax number from the address book or type one in.

If you want to send one fax to several people, you can keep adding them to the distribution list by clicking on '**Add to list**' after you type in a name and number. When you have entered all the names to which you want to send faxes, click on '**Next**'.

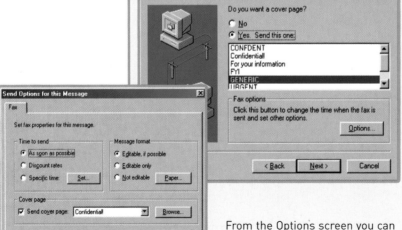

You can also send a cover page with your fax from a range of pre-designed templates. From this section you can also set some options (by clicking on the Options tab) concerning how to send your fax.

From the Options screen you can specify when to send a fax to take advantage of off-peak calling.

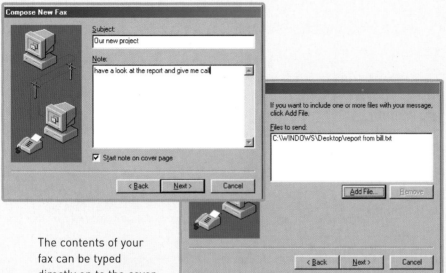

The contents of your fax can be typed directly on to the cover sheet or supplied from a separate text-based document. Click on **'Next'** to continue.

You can add many documents to the fax by simply clicking on '**Add File**' and selecting the documents you wish to fax. When you are ready, click on **'Next'** to continue.

Now the fax is ready to send. Clicking on **'Finish'** makes the fax software prepare to send. If you have specified a different time from 'soon as possible', the software waits and sends the fax at the time requested. You need to leave the PC on for the fax software to be able to send. If the line is engaged it will try again after a few minutes' interval.

At the appointed time, the software automatically attempts to send faxes. If the modem is in use, the fax will fail.

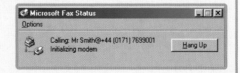

Extra software

The majority of modems bought as separate units come with additional software for sending and receiving faxes. This software is always superior to Windows' own fax software. Several shareware fax packages, including 'Just the fax' and 'MessageASAP', are available either free or at very low cost direct from Internet web sites specialising in shareware.

Warning!

Some types of documents may not be compatible with the faxing software. If you find a document will not fax properly, try converting it into either RTF (Rich Text Format) or BMP (Bitmap graphics file) and re-sending the document. The conversion process is normally carried out by using the application associated with the file and selecting 'Save As...', then changing the file type to either BMP or RTF.

INTRODUCING NEWSGROUPS

And now the weather . . .

Unlike the rest of the Internet, newsgroups are rarely affected by Internet weather (busy times that slow down data transfer rates). Most big ISPs host newsgroups on a local server and, as such, accessing them is just a single hop from you to your ISP.

Warning!

Newsgroups are notorious for viruses, pornography and foul language. To avoid such groups, look for ones described as 'moderated', but be aware that although this means that someone with the power to remove undesirable messages is watching this newsgroup, there is no guarantee that the moderator has the same value system as you.

Newsgroups are similar to electronic notice-boards, often used as an area where like-minded people can get together and discuss ideas, solve problems or just voice their opinions. Newsgroups are unregulated and may therefore contain text and pictures that are unsuitable for children. Some ISPs restrict or censor newsgroups for this reason.

Getting started

Of the various newsgroup readers, many are free and some come as part of email programs. This example shows Microsoft Outlook Express, which is a particularly common newsreader. When you connect for the first time you need to supply some details, the most important of which is the name of the news server to which you wish to attach. In most cases this will be called:

news.the_name_of_your_ISP.co.uk

You can also specify an email address and description of yourself so that other newsgroup users can reply to you directly.

If the newsreader requires any passwords or login names, you will need to contact your ISP for them.

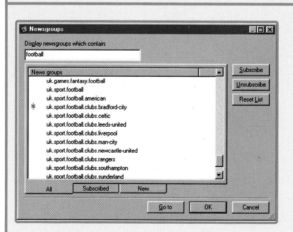

Searching for newsgroups

Once you are connected, the newsreader lists all the available newsgroups. This procedure can take quite a while as some servers have over 50,000 groups listed, on subjects ranging from

Typical newsreader software

1 Post a new message in this newsgroup

2 Replies can be sent either to the Author or the whole newsgroup

3 Allows you to search for a specific newsgroups or just browse amongst any that appeal to you

4 **Message display**: a small '+' next to one indicates that there are several responses from others. Clicking on the '+' displays the responses

5 Preview of the message you have selected. Messages can have attached documents. In this

package, an attached document is indicated by a paper clip in the top right-hand portion of the preview window. To save an attachment, use the File/Save As option on the menu bar

6 List of all the newsgroups to which you currently subscribe.

Speed tip

Newsgroups are great for meeting people and exchanging files. However, if you want some privacy you may have to invest in some additional software. The most common is PGP ('pretty good privacy'). The freeware versions of this technology allow you to encrypt data and files for both email and newsgroups. Only those who have a key and proper identification can unlock your data.

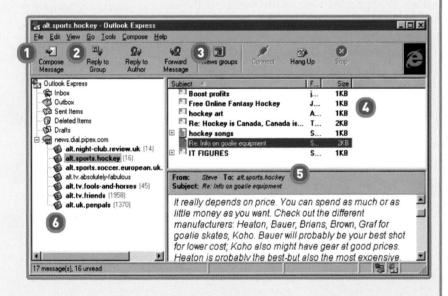

cookery to Japanese politics.

Newsgroup names follow a format similar to Internet web site names: e.g. alt.food.cooking.French is part of the ALTernative server under the folder Food, under the subfolder Cooking under the

subfolder French.

From this interface you can also do a search for newsgroups which contain a word which you have specified.

If you click on a group and select **'Subscribe'**, the name will be added to your newsgroup list for

convenient selection in the future.

If you select **'Go to'**, the software will attempt to download the headers in that group and then display them with just the header information.

CREATING YOUR OWN WEB SITE

Free — or almost

Most free space offers from ISPs come with a catch. In many cases you will have to take advertisement banners on your site or be prepared to sell your non-confidential user details to advertisers. Many of these web sites also have a limit on the number of Mb your site may contain. And if you need technical help, you may find you're out of luck.

Creating a web site is all the rage. Whether for business or pleasure, web site design is akin to desktop publishing (DTP). Like DTP software, many web-design programs use a simple cut-and-paste interface to lay out text and graphics. Most of the tools are free and many ISPs are providing web space at very low cost. This section looks at the four main steps for creating a web site.

STEP 1 Get some space for your web site from an Internet service provider (ISP).

Most ISPs now offer space on their servers for users to host their own web sites. Try doing a search on your ISP's home page, using phrases such as **'free web space'** or **'hosting a web page'**. If your ISP does not offer this service or it is expensive, try one of the many web sites that offer free hosting. In most cases you simply supply some details about yourself and choose a web address. For free sites, the suffix of the address will normally be that of the host, e.g. myhomepage@freeisp.co.uk.

Once you have signed up, you need a web creation program.

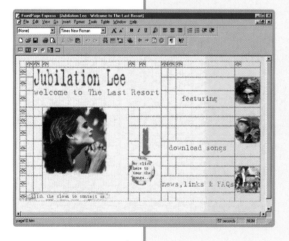

STEP 2 Design your web pages.

A web site is a bit like a tree, with a trunk from which sprout branches and leaves. The first page is called the **'home page'**, from which you can link to other pages, which can carry further links, and so on.

Every web site is created using HyperText Mark-up Language (HTML). To create a layered structure similar to the one on the left you can use software like that used for DTP, such as Microsoft Frontpage, Adobe PageMill and Netobject Fusion, which allows you to lay out text and graphics and create links to other pages. Many software packages for creating web sites are available free. To find

STEP 3 Upload your site from your local PC to your ISP's web server.

Your web-site creation software allows you to look at your web site while running on your PC. Once you are satisfied with the results, you need to upload to the web server that will be hosting your web site. To do this, you need a File Transfer Protocol program: wsftp and ftp explorer are both very popular FTP software packages and suitable for the beginner.

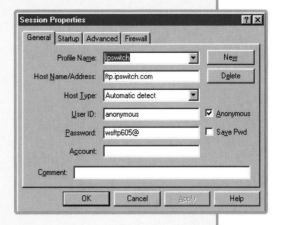

Before you can begin the upload, your FTP software needs to be set up with the address of the ISP hosting your web sites, your user name and password and possibly the name of the folder to which the files are going to be transferred. This information will be supplied to you by your ISP.

The FTP program, once given all the correct details such as user name, password and host address, connects to the Internet and attempts to upload any file you tell it to. Simply select the folder containing your web site from your local hard disk and send it to your Internet web space.

STEP 4 Improving your web site

Once you have uploaded your web site, you may have to wait a few hours while the ISP and the rest of the Internet recognises it. Once it is up, you can alter it simply by changing the index page to add more links for new pages and/or change graphics by redesigning the pages and uploading any changed files to the web site, making sure you use the same name as the old page. To add some spice to your web site you can add animations, sound — even links to other people's sites. If you want your own special web address — e.g. www.willshomepage.co.uk — you can get these from as little as £10 for two years. You do not have to change your web site: you just point this address to your web site.

You can also register with the search engines — this is free in most cases — by specifying a description of your site or by the search engine taking text from your site's first page and adding this into its database. If someone types into a search engine something that matches your site, it may display it on the search results page. The more unique a group of words you have, the better the chance of a successful search.

(STEP 2 continued)
one, go to a popular shareware Internet site such as download.com or use a search engine like Yahoo or Altavista. Then type in a phrase such as 'web page design' or 'HTML editor'. Whichever you choose, do not be afraid to experiment and do use the help system's instructions on how to use your chosen package.

Remember:
• make sure your first page is called 'Index'
• put all your individual pages and images in the same folder for ease of reference
• try to use compressed graphic files such as JPEG or Gif for pictures to reduce loading time for visitors.

A

ActiveX Software that enables Multimedia content from the Internet to be directly embedded in the Windows operating system

AGP (accelerated graphics port) An interface (q.v.) that enables your PC to use especially high-performance 3D graphics cards capable of displaying particularly complex images, notably in games

analogue/analog Means of electronic transmission. Analogue signals are continuous and can vary infinitesimally. A good example is the human voice, which is why telephone and broadcast communications were designed to use analogue technology. Early computers were analogue but all current PCs are digital (q.v.). A modem converts a signal from digital to analogue or *vice versa*, to enable digital computers to use analogue telephone lines

anti-virus software A special program designed to intercept viruses (destructive programs, q.v.) on your PC and stop them from causing harm or fix damage caused by viruses

API (application programming interface) A gateway or link within a program that allows other software to interact with it

applet A small program, especially one written in Java (q.v.) and downloaded from the Internet

application/application program Software that performs a specific function directly for the user or, in some cases, for another application program. Examples of applications include word processors, database programs, spreadsheets, web browsers, drawing, painting and image editing

Athlon A high-performance PC processor launched in 1999 by AMD as a competitor to Intel's market-leading Pentium III (q.v.) chip

attachment A file that is specially encoded and sent with an email (q.v.) message. An attachment, typically, is a file saved using a particular application (e.g. a word-processing program), so the recipient of the attachment must have an application capable of opening the file. This way of sending information preserves the format of the file — e.g. for a text document, the tabs, font sizes, etc.

AVI (audio video interleaved) A highly compressed sound and motion picture file for playback on a PC with suitable software. AVI players include Realvideo, RealPlayer, Microsoft Mediaplayer and Apple Quicktime. AVI files have the suffix .avi

B

backup A copy of a computer file made in case anything happens to the original. Backups can be made on hard disks, floppy disks, cartridges, computer tapes: in fact, on anything which allows you to have a second distinct copy

binary The base-two number system that computers use to represent digital data. '0' and '1' are the only binary digits; 2 in decimal (the base-ten number system) is represented as 10 in binary. The great advantage of a digital (q.v.) binary system is that the only possible values are simply the presence of a pulse (meaning 1) or its absence (meaning 0). The size of the pulse is not important

BIOS (Basic Input Output System) The BIOS stores fundamental information about the PC set-up (amount of memory, hard-disk size, etc.) and controls the PC when it starts up

bit The smallest unit of data used by a PC. Eight bits combine to make a byte, which is roughly one character of text

Bluetooth A new wireless standard for connecting electronic devices. Examples of appliances that use this technology are hands-free kits for mobile phones and digital cameras able to send pictures to desktop PCs

bookmark To record the address of an Internet site (because you may wish to return to it later). Bookmarking a site saves time because you have no need to key in its address

bootup The start-up procedure for a PC. Controlled by the BIOS (q.v.), it starts the computer, finds an operating system (OS, q.v.), then passes on basic information about the system to the OS

bps (bits per second) A common measure of speed for data communications. The speed of transmission via a modem (q.v.) is often measured in this way

browser A program used for navigating the World Wide Web. The two most common browsers are Microsoft Internet Explorer and Netscape Navigator

bubblejet printer *See* inkjet printer

bug A coding error in a computer program which may cause the program to behave erratically

button A small panel on the screen image showing words such as 'OK' or 'Cancel'. Press on the button (with the mouse) to make your choice

byte Comprising eight bits (q.v.) of computer data, a byte is roughly equivalent to one character of text

C

cabinet (CAB) file A single computer file created to hold a number of compressed files. A set of cabinet files can be contained in a folder. During the installation of a program, the compressed files in a cabinet are decompressed and copied to an appropriate directory for the user. Cabinet files are similar to the ZIP file standard. A cabinet file usually carries the suffix '.cab'

cache A storage device for frequently used information which reduces the time an application takes to access information. For instance, a web browser stores pages visited on your disk, so that if you visit them again it has only to check for changes, as most of the information is already in your computer. RAM cache is extra-fast memory for storing data until the processor needs it

CAD (computer-aided design) Special software used by architects, engineers, draughtsmen, artists and others to create precision drawings and technical illustrations. CAD software can be used to create two-dimensional (2D) drawings or three-dimensional (3D) models

CD-ROM Compact disk read-only memory: a CD, of the same size and shape as an audio CD, that can hold up to 650Mb of computer data (text, pictures, movies etc.). CD-ROMs are read in a special CD-ROM drive which can also play music CDs but cannot write to any CDs. CD drives are being superseded by DVD (q.v.) drives, which use disks that can store much higher volumes

CD writer A special type of CD-ROM drive which allows you to write to blank CDs. The two types of disks are CDRs, which can be written to once, and CD-RWs, which can be written to over and over again

Celeron A budget range of PC processors from Intel (q.v.)

chip A tiny piece of semiconductor material, such as silicon, processed for use in an integrated circuit or component

chipset The chips used on the motherboard of a PC to allow the processor to talk to other PC components such as the memory and hard disk

client A requesting program or user in a client/server system — e.g. the user of a web browser (q.v.), who makes requests, as a client, for pages from servers on the Internet. The browser itself is a client in the context of its relationship with the computer from which it is getting information

clip art Ready-made drawings or illustrations, arranged by category, that can be freely copied by cutting and pasting into your own documents. Clip art often comes free with applications which can use it (such as word-processing and presentation software), but themed packages are also available

clock speed The speed at which a PC processor can deal with instructions — e.g. a clock speed of 700MHz means that the chip can handle 700 million sets of instructions every second

codec (coder/decoder or compression/decompression) Used to describe software, integrated circuits, or chips that perform data conversion. In this context, the term is an acronym for 'coder/decoder'. This type of codec combines analogue-to-digital conversion and digital-to-analogue conversion functions in a single chip or via a software application

COM1, COM2, COM3 The common names for the PC's serial connections, used for modems, printers, etc. *See* serial communication

compression Reduction of the space taken up by a file by encoding the data in it more efficiently

control panel The command centre for Windows and other operating systems. You can use it to set and access options for your printer, soundcard, graphics card and much more

cookie Information stored on your hard disk by a web site. It may include a user name and your own preferences, so that the next time you visit it is customised for you

copy A command which lets you copy information from one document to another (which may be controlled by the same or a different application)

CPU (central processing unit) Also called processor (q.v.) or microprocessor. The principal chip inside a PC, which provides most of its power and directs how all its functions are carried out

crash Malfunction of a program or the PC itself signalled by the screen freezing. The cause may be trivial and the easiest cure may be to restart the PC

CRT (cathode-ray tube) The core of a monitor, this is a vacuum-filled cone with a phosphor coating on the inside of the screen. Controlled by the PC's graphics card, an electron gun fires electrons at the screen, where they make the phosphor glow to create the image. Flat screens, used in laptop computers, use different technology and not CRTs

cut A command which lets you move a selected section of a document to a clipboard from which you can paste it into another document

D

DAT (digital audio tape) A standard medium for the digital recording (of professional quality) of sound on tape. A DAT drive is a digital tape-recorder which can record at sample rates of up to 48KHz, greater even than the CD audio standard. Digital inputs and outputs on professional DAT decks allow the user to transfer recordings from the DAT tape to an audio workstation for precise editing. The compact size and low cost of the DAT medium makes it an excellent way to compile recordings that are going to be used to create a CD master

database A program for storing information on a PC in a structured format which enables you to determine the relationships between different items of data as well as offering powerful search capabilities. A simple database is like a card-index file which can be viewed by any item in any order

defrag/defragmentation The process of cleaning up a hard disk by shuffling all the contents of the disk so that each file is stored neatly in one area and all the empty space is together too. This speeds up data retrieval. *See also* fragmentation

desktop The first Windows screen you see when your PC has finished running through the start-up routine. Made to resemble a real desktop, it displays icons (q.v.) that provide shortcuts to programs and data files

dialogue/dialog box A message window, displayed by Windows or by a program, and demanding some sort of response from the user

digital Means of electronic transmission via signals that comprise separate pulses, each of which can take only one of a set of specific values. Early computers used the alternative analogue (q.v.) technology. Digital computers proved much more reliable; hence, all current PCs are digital

digital camera A camera which records photos in memory rather than on film, so you can download pictures straight to your PC. It uses a light-sensitive panel to convert images into a computer file

DIMM (dual in-line memory module) A module containing several RAM (q.v.) chips on a small circuit board with pins that connect it to the computer's motherboard (q.v.). A DIMM has a 168-pin connector and supports 64-bit data transfer. DIMM is by far the most common type of computer memory

directory Also known as a folder, this is a structure or area for keeping files together on a disk. Folders can be nested inside other folders, which are themselves inside other folders

DirectX Developed by Microsoft, DirectX is a range of multimedia add-ons for Windows. In theory, it allows games developers and hardware designers to ensure that all their products work together

DOS (disk operating system) A basic PC operating system (q.v.) that uses typed commands rather than the graphics of Windows. Windows is based on DOS

dot-matrix printer Machine which makes up text and images from dots created by striking tiny pins against an inked ribbon, much like a typewriter. Now largely superseded by inkjet and laser printers but sometimes used with carbon-copy forms, e.g. for multi-part invoice printing

download To transfer files or data to a PC, either from the Internet or from another device such as a digital camera

dpi (dots per inch) A measure of the sharpness (i.e. the density of illuminated points) on a display screen or printer. The dpi for a given screen resolution varies according to the overall size of the screen

drag and drop A way of moving a highlighted file or selected part of a document by clicking and holding the mouse button, then dragging the selection to a new location and dropping it by releasing the button

driver A small program needed for making a specific computer accessory, such as a printer, work properly with a PC

DTP (desktop publishing) The design and layout of magazines, books and other documents using a computer. DTP software gives the user great control over layout and flexibility in printing

DVD (digital versatile disk) A DVD looks like a CD but uses a different type of laser with improved media and can hold up to 17Gb of data — more than enough for a full-length movie. A DVD drive can play CDs but a CD drive cannot use DVDs

E

email (electronic mail) A means of sending messages and file attachments from one computer to another across the Internet or a local network

ethernet A standard for linking computers together to form a local network, generally in an office environment

execute (executable and .EXE files) To execute a program is to run it on a computer. In Windows 98, program file names normally include the suffix .EXE

expansion card A small circuit board that can be plugged into the motherboard (q.v.) of a computer to add more functions to it. Examples include modems, network cards and soundcards

expansion slot The electrical connector on the motherboard (q.v.) into which an expansion card is plugged

extension Suffix: the three letters after the dot in a PC filename; typically, they indicate the type or format of the file

F

FAQ (frequently asked question) A common abbreviation, used on web sites, newsgroups, etc. to describe a page or a file which tries to answer the most common – and obvious – questions about the site. This saves you time as you can find the answers quickly, and also saves the web site staff or newsgroup regulars from answering the same questions over and over again

favorite The name given by Internet Explorer (q.v.) for an Internet site you visit often — 'bookmarked' (q.v.) — so you can jump to it from a list rather than having to type in its address every time

file extension See extension

FireWire A super-fast data link between the PC and external devices, mainly digital camcorders at present. The generic term for this technology is the IEEE1394 standard

flatbed scanner A scanner that looks like the top half of a photocopier. The document (text or picture) is placed face-down on a sheet of glass for scanning and is then stored as a file on the PC

floppy disk A small removable disk holding up to 1.44Mb of data which can be used for storing files or for transferring them from one PC to another

font A particular design or style of typeface, e.g. Times, Helvetica, Univers

format To prepare a completely blank disk so that the operating system can write information to it. Essentially, it provides an address for each physical part of the disk so that the PC can find the information again

fragmentation A new hard disk writes each new file to a virgin area. As files are amended (being increased or reduced in size, re-saved or deleted), the stored data gets dispersed to different locations on the disk (fragmented), the various items of data being reunited when you retrieve the file. This process of joining the data together again slows down the PC; defragmentation (q.v.) cleans up the disk and improves performance by moving the segments of files back together

FTP (file transfer protocol) A method of transferring files from one computer to another across the Internet. FTP is commonly used to download large files or to load documents into a web site

G

Gb (gigabyte) A measurement of storage space equal to 1,024Mb

GIF (graphics interchange format) A type of graphics file commonly used to display images on the Internet

graphics card The part of a PC that controls what is displayed on screen

GUI (graphical user interface) A method of driving software by means of windows, menus, buttons, icons and so on. For example, while DOS (q.v.) uses only text, Windows — a GUI system — uses pictures to show you what is happening on the screen

H

hacking A slang term for gaining unauthorised access to other people's computer systems and networks, or for making unauthorised changes to software programs

hard disk A magnetic storage device capable of holding huge amounts of data. It is used in a PC to hold Windows, programs and users' files

hardware The computer and its peripherals (q.v.): the tangible part of a computer's set-up. Programs are known as software

homepage The first, introductory page seen by visitors to a web site

HTML (hypertext mark-up language) A coded language used to describe how a web page should look. When the page is loaded into a browser such as Netscape Navigator or Internet Explorer (q.v.), the browser interprets the HTML and displays the page correctly

hyperlink A clickable link or hotspot which lets you jump between web sites, documents, or places in a document

I

icon A tiny symbol displayed on screen to represent an application, file or command

IDE (integrated drive electronics) The most common standard for connecting hard disks, CD-ROM drives etc. in a PC. Alternatives include the faster, but more expensive, SCSI (q.v.)

image editing The process of manipulating or altering photos or illustrations on a PC, using applications such as PhotoShop, PaintShop Pro or Corel Draw

infrared port A means of connecting a PC to other devices and computers, transmitting data using infrared light rather than using wires; similar to the port on a television that receives instructions from the remote control buttons

inkjet printer One that squirts precisely controlled droplets of ink on to the paper to build up the image. Although they are relatively cheap, modern inkjet printers can produce pictures that are almost indistinguishable from photographs. However, they are slow and the ink these printers use is expensive. Some manufacturers use the term 'bubblejet' instead of 'inkjet'

Intel Maker of the 8086, 80286 and Pentium ranges of processors which are used in IBM PCs and compatible computers

interface Design feature that allows different electronic devices to communicate with each other. Programs interact with their users by means of a 'user interface', defined by its 'look and feel' and overall design. The standards by which peripherals and PC components communicate with the computer itself are also known as interfaces

Internet International network of computers. Developed from US military and academic networks, the Internet is now easily accessible from most computers on company networks or computers connected to telephone lines via modems

Internet Explorer A popular web browser included in the Windows 98 package and which also works closely with Windows 95

Interrupt ReQuest (IRQ) An assigned location where the computer can expect a device to interrupt it when the device sends the computer signals about its operation. For example, when a printer has finished printing, it sends an interrupt signal to the computer. The signal momentarily interrupts the computer so that it can decide what processing to do next. Since multiple signals to the computer on the same interrupt line might not be understood by the computer, a unique value must be specified for each device and its path to the computer. Devices can share IRQ, although this can sometimes cause an error or a conflict

intranet Internal computer network used within an organisation

IRC (Internet Relay Chat) A means of 'chatting' to other Internet users using real-time typed messages

ISA (industry standard architecture) A slot design found in older PCs for attaching expansion cards so that devices such as a screen or soundcard can be added to the system. Modern PCs are more likely to use the newer slot design, PCI (q.v.)

ISDN (integrated services digital network) A digital telephone line that allows you to send and receive data more quickly than a normal telephone connection. It is used for high-volume direct data transfer and for Internet access

ISP (Internet service provider) Although it is possible to connect a computer directly to the Internet, this is too expensive for most companies and home users. Instead, an ISP connects its computers to the Internet and then allows its customers (both corporate and domestic) to connect to these, thus linking to the Net indirectly

J

Java A special programming language used chiefly on web sites to add sophisticated animations and interactive effects

joystick A device that lets you control movement, especially in computer games

JPEG (joint picture experts group) A type of graphics file, commonly used to display images on the Internet or for presentations. It can be very highly compressed so the pictures take up less space

jumpers These connect the little metal pins found on expansion cards (q.v.) and PC motherboards (q.v.), allowing you to change settings manually

K

K56flex An early 56Kbits/sec modem technology. If your modem is a K56flex model, ensure that it can be upgraded to the modern V90 standard (q.v.)

K6, K6-2, K6-III PC processors made by AMD (American Micro Devices), a major rival to Intel in the CPU market

Kb (kilobyte) A unit of data, equal to 1,024 bytes (q.v.). This is enough to store just over 1,000 characters of text

Kbits/sec (kilobits per second; kbps) A measure of data transfer speed, often used to compare modem specifications (8Kbits = 1Kb)

L

LAN (local area network) Network of computers that are physically near each other, e.g. in the same office

laptop computer Small (telephone-directory-size) portable computer that can be used away from a power source. Laptops are much more expensive than desktop computers

laser printer A type of printer which uses a laser beam to generate high-quality text and graphics. Black and white laser printers are generally affordable but colour models remain expensive

li-ion (lithium ion) The most sophisticated type of rechargeable battery, used in many notebook computers (q.v.). It is light and offers very high power capacity, but is expensive

login The process of connecting a computer to a network or to an ISP (q.v.). The user name you enter in order to identify yourself is also called a login

LPT1, LPT2 The DOS names (from 'line printer') for the PC's parallel connections, used for printers, scanners and disk drives. *See* parallel communication

LS-120 A type of disk drive that can store 120Mb of data on a single disk of the same size as a floppy disk. The drives can also read and write to normal floppies

M

Macintosh (popularly, 'Mac') Introduced in 1984 by Apple Computer, this was the first widely sold personal computer with a graphical user interface (GUI) (q.v.)

Mb (megabyte) A measure of computer processor storage and real and virtual memory; one Mb is 1,048,576 bytes (q.v.)

Mbps (millions of bits per second, or **megabits per second)** A measure of band width, or data-carrying capacity, representing the total information flow over a second: hence, speed of transmission of data — between computers, between computer and printer, around the Internet, and so on

microprocessor *See* processor

modem (modulator/demodulator) A device that modulates ingoing and outgoing signals from a computer or other digital device for transmission over conventional copper twisted-pair telephone lines. It superimposes a digital (q.v.) data signal over a carrier to enable the computer data to travel over an analogue (q.v.) telephone line, and the modem at the other end extracts the data from the carrier so that it can travel digitally again

monitor The piece of computer equipment that provides the screen

motherboard The physical base that contains the computer's basic circuitry and components. Common components on a motherboard include CPU, RAM and ISA/PCI interface sockets (q.v.)

MPEG (moving picture experts group) A standard for digital video and digital audio compression. The most common standards for video are MPEG Video and MP3 Audio

MP3 (MPEG-1 audio layer-3) A standard technology and format for compressing a sound sequence into a very small file while preserving the original level of sound quality

multimedia Combined use of media (e.g. sound, graphics, video, text)

N

Net See Internet

Netscape Web browser, available as Navigator or the more recent Communicator, and the company that developed it

NetWare A provider of software and protocols for networking between servers and clients' PCs; part of the Novell Corporation

network Group of computers linked together so that they can share files and resources such as printers and Internet access

newsgroups International discussion areas on the Internet, covering a huge range of topics

notebook computer Similar to, but slightly smaller than, a laptop computer (q.v.)

O

OpenGL (open graphics library) The computer industry's standard application program interface (API) for defining 2-D and 3-D graphic images

operating system The software that controls the computer and provides basic functions for applications (e.g. allows word processor to open and save files). Microsoft Windows is the most commonly used operating system

P

parallel communication One of two traditional standards (the other being serial, q.v.) for transmitting data. *See* LPT1, LPT2

PCI (peripheral component interconnect) A slot design for connecting expansion cards to a PC

PCMCIA (Personal Computer Memory Card International Association) Sometimes called PC card, this is a standard for a credit-card-sized memory or input-output device that fits into a notebook or laptop computer

PDA (personal digital assistant) A small, hand-held device that provides computing facilities, and information storage and retrieval for personal or business users, usually for keeping track of schedules and addresses

Pentium, Pentium II, Pentium III The Pentium is the most common processor (q.v.) for desktop computers. First produced in 1993 by Intel (q.v.), the Pentium quickly replaced Intel's 486 processor as the microchip of choice. The Pentium III is faster than the Pentium II

peripherals Hardware items separate from the PC, such as printers, screens (monitors) and scanners

PGP (pretty good privacy) A system for securing documents by means of encryption

pixel Derived from 'picture element', this is the basic unit of programmable colour on a computer display or in a computer image

plug-and-play See PnP

PnP (plug-and-play) A technology that gives computer users the ability to plug a device into a computer and have the computer recognise it automatically

port Socket

PowerPC A microprocessor architecture developed jointly by Apple, IBM and Motorola used in Apple Macintosh computers and some IBM computers. The PowerPC is the Pentium's main competitor

processor/microprocessor The 'engine' of any PC: the silicon chip that does all the work, e.g. Pentium, PowerPC. *See also* CPU

program *See* application

protocol A special set of rules for communicating between computer systems

Q

QWERTY A keyboard with a top row of letter keys starting Q,W,E,R,T,Y

R

registry (Windows Registry, Internet Registry) In the Microsoft Windows operating systems, the registry is a single location for keeping such information as devices attached, system options and what application programs are to be loaded when the operating system is stored

Registered Jacks (RJ-11, RJ-14, RJ-45) A series of telephone connection interfaces registered with the United States Federal Communications Commission. The USA, Europe and Asia all have different jack types. RJ-45 plugs and sockets are generally used in ethernet networks (q.v.)

RAM (random access memory) Memory that can be read from and written to; usually expressed in megabytes (q.v.), e.g. 8Mb

reset To restart the PC either by pressing the reset button or using the Ctrl+Alt+Del combination of keys. Also known as a 'warm boot', as the power is not turned off. A reset is often used after a system crash (q.v.), but only if normal restart methods are unsuccessful as resetting can lose unsaved data or corrupt files

ROM (read-only memory) Storage device that holds data permanently and may not be changed by the programmer

S

screen saver Moving graphic which appears on the monitor after a set period of time; open applications are still active. If a CRT-based monitor is left with the same image displayed for a long time, the image begins to burn in (so that you still see that image when the screen is turned off). To stop this happening, screen savers always have moving pictures

scroll bar Strip that appears along the right side and/or bottom of a window when the document contains more than can be displayed in the window, with arrows allowing you to 'scroll' up, down or across the document

SCSI (small computer system interface) Developed at Apple Computers, this is a set of standard electronic interfaces that allow personal computers to communicate with peripheral hardware such as disk drives, tape drives, CD-ROM drives, printers and scanners faster and more flexibly than previous interfaces. *See also* IDE

search engine Means of searching the Internet, e.g. Yahoo, Lycos, Altavista

sector Defined portion of a disk

serial communication One of two traditional standards (the other being parallel) for transmitting data. *See* COM1, COM2

server In a network (q.v.) of computers, the computer that has the main hard-disk or storage for the other machines. In some networks, the server will also run applications for clients attached to it, passing information to the client on request

shareware Software that is distributed free on a trial basis in the hope that the user may want to buy it later

shortcut key Key combination that allows you to carry out a particular command quickly, e.g. Ctrl+Esc brings up the task list (q.v.)

software Series of programs that tell the computer what to do, e.g. WordPerfect and Word for word processing, Excel for spreadsheets

spreadsheet Application used for arithmetical calculations such as budgets, costings and quotations

status bar A display at the bottom of a window that shows information about a process, function or selected item

subdirectory (or folder) A subdivision of the files on a disk

T

task list A pop-up menu displaying all of the currently running applications

TCP/IP (transmission control protocol/Internet protocol) The standard used by every PC to enable it to move information around the Internet, so that NetWare, Unix, Windows and Apple computers can all communicate with each other. The network control panel includes TCP/IP settings which may prevent Internet access unless they are set correctly

Telnet An Internet service, used for computer games involving many participants, that allows you to log on to a computer somewhere else via the Internet and use it as if you were sitting in front of it

title bar Part of a window or dialog box that shows the name of either the application running in the window or the dialog box. The title bar in the currently selected window is a different colour from those for inactive windows

toggle Item that can be selected or deselected with the same action

U

UNIX Computer operating system (q.v.) designed to be used by many people at the same time (as in companies, organisations, universities or groups maintained by ISPs)

upload To transfer files from your PC to another (opposite of download, q.v.)

URL (uniform resource locator) The address of a web page

USB (universal serial bus) Standard for transmitting data that is faster than traditional serial or parallel communication. Modern PCs incorporate USB sockets so that expansion cards are not necessary. Devices connected by USB can be added or removed without the need to turn the PC off (i.e. hot-swapping)

utility Tool for making a specific task easier (e.g. mail-merge or email software) or for fixing problems

V

version Updated and 'improved' edition of a software package, often denoted by a higher number

VGA (video graphics adapter) This has come to mean the standard 15-pin socket used to connect a screen (monitor) to the computer

virus Destructive program specially designed to 'infect' and usually damage other applications. It can alter and delete data and cause serious computer system malfunctions

W

wallpaper Graphic image, the colour and pattern of which can be varied, displayed on desktop background. As documents are created, the wallpaper disappears until the user returns to the desktop

WAP (wireless application protocol) Standard for transmitting data between mobile phones and special Internet sites

warm boot *See* reset

web site Set of themed pages on the World Wide Web (q.v.)

window Framed area on the screen in which you run applications and perform tasks. A window can be opened, closed, resized and moved

Windows (Microsoft Windows) Picture-based software which uses pull-down menus, dialog boxes and mouse-oriented operation. It was designed to make IBM PCs more user-friendly

Windows NT The business version of Windows, designed to be more efficient, reliable and internally secure

word processing Application (q.v.) for handling text, allowing corrections to be made, and font/type size to be changed, spelling to be checked and words counted before the document is printed out

work station Single-user microcomputer; or, in a LAN, a PC that serves a single user

World Wide Web (WWW) International network of computers which provides information and services in the form of web sites (q.v.). Most small users who want their own web site use a professional host (an ISP, q.v.) so that their site is available all the time

Z

ZIP A file extension (q.v.) for files compressed by the program PKZIP

NUMERIC TERMS

286, 386, 486 Types of PC processor developed by Intel (q.v.) used in PCs before the Pentium chip (q.v.) was introduced. PCs using these chips are now becoming outdated

3D graphics Images which appear to have depth and are much more realistic than flat (two-dimensional) ones; they demand a powerful PC and graphics card. 3D graphics are used in games and multimedia software, as well as in professional design packages

56Kbits/sec The current fastest speed for a modem (q.v.) is shown as 56Kbits/sec, meaning that 56 kilobits of data per second can be sent down a phone line

Over 2,000 recognised file types are currently used by PC systems. In addition there are a number of file formats of programs which are no longer produced. The Internet has many places to download information stored as files. If you download a file which will not open via your favourite application, use this chart to find out what the file does and what application created it.

A

ABK Corel Draw AutoBackup
ABR Brush file (Adobe PhotoShop)
ABS MPEG Audio Sound file
ACAD Database file (AutoCAD)
ACB ACBM Graphic image
ACE Archiver Compression file
ACF Adobe custom filter (Adobe PhotoShop)
ACL Corel Draw 6 keyboard accelerator file
ACM Windows system directory file
ACO Colour Palette (Adobe PhotoShop)
ADF Amiga disk file
ADI AutoCAD device-independent binary plotter file
AFP Graphics file (IBM)
AIF Audio Interchange File for Macintosh applications
AMF Music file (Advanced Module Format)
ANI Microsoft Windows Animated cursor
ANS ANSI Text file
ART Clip Art
ASC ASCII Text file
ASF Microsoft Advanced Streaming Format
ASP Active Server Page
ASX Video file
ATM Adobe Type Manager data/info file
AU Audio U-law (pronounced mu-law)
AVI Microsoft Audio Video Interleaved file
AWD FaxView Document image

B

BAT Batch file
BDB Microsoft Works Dababase file
BFC Windows 95 Briefcase Document
BKS Microsoft Works Spreadsheet Backup
BMP Windows or OS/2 bitmap

C

CDA CD Audio Track
CDB Clipboard file
CHK File fragments saved by scan /defrag
COM Command file (program)
CPD Fax cover document

D

DAT Data file
DBW Microsoft Windows 9.x Database file
DCS Bitmap Graphics (Quark XPress)
DDB Bitmap Graphics file
DIB Device-independent bitmap
DIC Dictionary file
DOC WordStar document
DOC WordPerfect document
DOC Microsoft Word document
DOC DisplayWrite document
DOS Text file (DOS)
DOT Word Document Template (Microsoft Word for Windows)
DRV Device Driver (required to make a device function)

E

EML Microsoft Outlook Express mail message (MIME RFC 822)
EPS Encapsulated Postscript Vector graphics (Adobe Illustrator)
EPS Encapsulated PostScript image file
EPS Printer font (Epson, Xerox, Ventura Publisher)
EPSF Encapsulated PostScript
EXE Executable file

F

FAQ Frequently Asked Questions document
FAX Type image
FLI FLIC animation (AutoDesk)
FP3 FileMaker Pro database

G

GIF Bitmap (CompuServe)
GSM Audio stream Raw GSM (6.10 audio stream)

H

HLP Help file (Generic)
HTM A Web page (Hypertext Markup Language)

HTML A Web page (Hypertext Markup Language)

I

ICC Printer file (Kodak)
ICM Image Color Matching profile
ICO Icon (Microsoft Windows 3.x)
INF Install script (generic)
INI Initialisation file (generic)

J

JFF JPEG Image
JIF JPEG Image
JFIF JPEG Image
JPE JPEG Image
JPEG Compressed bitmap
JPG JPEG Bitmap

K

KEY Security file (such as a software registration number)
KYB Keyboard mapping (FTP)

L

LHA Compressed Archive (LHA/LHARC)
LWP Wordpro 96/97 file (Lotus)
LZH Compressed archive (LH ARC)

M

MDB Database (Microsoft Access)
MDL Model file (Quake)
MMF Mail message file (Microsoft Mail)
MME A multipart file in the Multi-Purpose Internet Mail Extensions (MIME) format
MOV Movie (QuickTime for Microsoft Windows)
MOV Movie (AutoCAD/AutoFlix)
MP2 MPEG Audio Layer 2
MP3 MPEG Audio Layer 3 (AC3)
MPEG Animation
MPG MPEG Animation
MSP Paint bitmap (Microsoft)

N

NSF Database (Lotus Notes)
NWS News message (Microsoft Outlook Express)

O

123 Lotus 1-2-3, '97 data file
ORG Calendar file (Lotus Organizer)
OR2 Calendar file (Lotus Organizer 2)
OR3 Lotus Organizer 97 file

P

PBM Portable bitmap graphic
PCM Audio file
PCW Text file (PC Write)
PCX PC Paintbrush bitmap (ZSoft)
PDF Portable Document file (Adobe Acrobat)
PGP Encrypted file
PKR Public Keyring (PGP)
PM6 Document (PageMaker 6.0)
PNT Graphic file (MacPaint)
PPT PowerPoint presentation (Microsoft)
PUB Publication (Ventura Publisher)
PUB Document (Microsoft Publisher)
PUB Public key ring file (PGP)
PWL Password list file (Microsoft Windows 9.x)

Q

QRY Query (Microsoft)
QT Movie file (QuickTime)
QTI Image file (QuickTime)
QTIF Image file (QuickTime)
QTM Movie file (QuickTime)

R

RAM Metafile (RealAudio)
RAS Bitmap (Sun Raster Images)
REM Remarks file (generic)
RIF RIFF Bitmap graphics (Fractal Design Painter)
RIF Image file (Metacreations Painter 5)
RLE Run-Length Encoded bitmap
RTF Rich Text Format document

S

SAM Document (AMI Professional)

T

TIF Tag image bitmap file (TIFF)
TIFF Tag image bitmap file (TIFF)
TXT ASCII text-formatted audio data

V

VBS Script file (Microsoft Visual Basic)
VOX Audio file (Talking Technology)

W

WK1 Spreadsheet (Lotus 1-2-3 v. 1 and 2)
WK3 Spreadsheet (Lotus 1-2-3 v. 3)
WK4 Spreadsheet (Lotus 1-2-3 v. 4)
WKB Document file (Microsoft WordPerfect for Windows)
WKS Worksheet spreadsheet (Lotus 1-2-3)
WKS Document (Microsoft Works)
WMF Metafile (Microsoft Windows)
WP Document file (Microsoft WordPerfect for Windows)
WPA Word processor document
WP4 Document (Microsoft WordPerfect for Windows 4.0)
WP5 Document (Microsoft WordPerfect for Windows 5.0)
WP6 Document (Microsoft WordPerfect for Windows 6.0
WPS Text document (Microsoft Works)
WRI Write document (Windows Write)
WS7 Document (WordStar for Windows version 7)
WSD Document (WordStar for Windows 2000)

X

XLB Datafile (Microsoft Excel)
XLC Chart file (Microsoft Excel)
XML eXtensible markup language
XLS Spreadsheet (Microsoft Excel)

Z

ZIP Zip file Compressed archive

The Internet has many thousands of sites holding information that could be useful to you as a PC user. The listings that follow are, however, only suggestions — not recommended sites. By using a search engine such as Altavista, Excite or Yahoo you can find useful technology web sites for yourself.

BUYING GUIDES AND PRODUCT REVIEWS

www.css.msu.edu/pc-guide.html
One of the best web sites for the PC enthusiast, though heavily American (in terms of language, suppliers and prices), this is non-profit-making and advertisement-free. Note that some of the information is out of date

www.dealtime.co.uk
Good for finding computer bargains

www.gamespot.com
Popular with video-game fans

www.hardwarecentral.com
News and reviews of the latest hardware

www.internetsourcebook.com
Useful for information on computer companies. Strong US bias

www.itreviews.co.uk
News, reviews and technical guides for UK users

www.reviewbooth.com
An aggregated review service covering over 10,000 computer products

www.sharkyextreme.com
Famous site for the PC enthusiast and gadget freak

www.techweb.com/shopper
Another long-established site with many informative guides to computer technology, but heavy on advertising

TECHNOLOGY NEWS

A good collection of web sites dedicated to providing the latest news from the world of technology.

Many are US-focused, but try substituting '.co.uk' for 'com' in case there is a more UK-centric version. Some sites may even have links on their home pages to equivalent UK sites.

www.businesswire.com

www.cmpnet.com

www.cnet.com

www.computerreview.com

www.idg.net

www.internetnews.com

www.newshub.com

www.newsbytes.com

www.herring.com

www.techserver.com

www.techweb.com

www.upside.com

www.wired.com

www.zdnet.com/zdnn

CONSUMER ADVICE

www.tradingstandards.gov.uk
Useful site covering current trading standards

www.trustuk.org.uk
Government-backed, non-profit-making scheme to help online consumers by regulating Internet codes of practice

MOTHERBOARD AND PC COMPONENT MANUFACTURERS

These sites may have a UK equivalent under the .co.uk suffix.

HARD DISK
www.quantum.com

www.seagate.com

www.wdc.com

MOTHERBOARDS
www.abit.com.tw

www.asus.com.tw

www.a-trend.com

www.giga-byte.com

www.intel.com

www.micronics.com

www.motherboard.com

www.supermicro.com

MICROPROCESSORS
www.amd.com

www.cyrix.com

www.digital.com

www.ibm.com

www.intel.com

ANTI-VIRUS SOFTWARE VENDORS

Central Command Software
Products: AVP (Antiviral Toolkit Pro)
www.centralcommand.com

Frisk Software
Products: F-Prot
www.complex.is

Kaspersky Labs
Products: AVP (Antiviral Toolkit Pro)
www.avp.ru

Network Associates
Products: VirusScan, NetShield
www.nai.com

Norman Data Defense Systems
Products: Norman Virus Control
www.norman.no

Panda Software
Products: Panda AntiVirus
www.pandasoftware.com

StarLabs
Virus-scanning service at ISP level
www.starlabs.net

Sophos
Products: DFence, AntiVirus
www.sophos.com

Symantec Corporation
Products: Norton Anti-Virus
www.symantec.com

Trend Micro
Products: PC-cillin, InterScan VirusWall
www.antivirus.com

CLASSIFIED ADS (FOR USED PARTS)

www.ebay.com
The world's largest multi-purpose online
auction with a large technology section

www.loot.co.uk
Online version of the British free-ads
paper

TROUBLESHOOTING AND TIPS
FOR UPGRADING PCS

Many of these sites are very technical and
offer limited direct technical support.
However, they carry a lot of useful
information.

www.anandtech.com
For PC enthusiasts. Very technical but
often first with niche-product reviews and
information

www.computerwire.com
Useful business site but quite expensive
for the home user

www.helpanswers.com
A useful problem-solver for common
Windows errors

www.motherboards.org
A site dedicated to PC motherboards.
Useful for upgrading and troubleshooting
PC systems

www.pcguide.com
Famous techies' site, full of useful guides

www.sysopt.com
Tips for tweaking your PC. Quite
technical, so use with caution

www.techweb.com
General news-and-reviews technology
web site. Mostly US-focused

www.tomshardware.com
Another web site from a long-serving and
notorious PC enthusiast. Packed with
useful information but very technical

www.wired.com
Online magazine about the Internet

http://www.zdnet.co.uk/pcdir/bg/
Buyer's guide for PC hardware and
software

Index

VDU (visual display unit) see screen
VGA connector 31, 180
video editing 139
viruses 48-9, 119, 180
  anti-virus software 48, 49, 118, 148, 174
  email and 49, 162
  macro viruses 48
  newsgroups 170
  payloads 48
  self-replicating viruses 48
  Trojans 48, 49
volume control 37, 102

Wake on LAN/modem ring option 117
WAP (wireless application protocol) 157, 180
warranties 9, 10-11, 112
  collect and return warranty (C&R) 10
  cover 10-11
  extended warranties 10, 11
  invalidating 40, 152
  manufacturers' telephone helplines 10
  onsite warranty 10
  repair turnaround time 10
  return to base (RTB)

warranty 10
and upgrades 138
the Web 157, 181
  integration into PC desktop 68-9
web servers 173
web sites 172-3, 180, 184-5
  addresses 63, 158
  creating 172-3
  design 172-3
  display settings 166
  free web space 172
  FTP (File Transfer Protocol) 173, 177
  graphics 173
  HTML (HyperText Mark-up Language) 172, 177
  improving 173
  links 158, 173
  mirror sites 164
  search facility 159
  storing images from 159
  uploading to web server 173
web addresses 173
wildcard searches 57
Windows 180
  customisation 60-83
  desktop see desktop
  help system 25, 34
  operating system 15, 22-3,

115
problems 37
quirks 86, 87
re-installing 130-1
tour guide 23
updating 104-5
utilities 34-5
Windows 95 6, 12, 24
Windows 98 6, 12, 14
Windows 2000 6, 12, 24
Windows key 21
Windows Recovery disk 119
Windows Schemes 78-9
Windows Setup utility 29
WinZip 165
Word
  spell-checker 106
  text repositioning 107
  troubleshooting 106-7
word processing 8, 114, 180
WordPad 26
work area 26

Yahoo 173

z-buffering 111
Zip drives 7, 75, 125, 153
Zip files 165, 181

Which? Books are commissioned and researched by
Consumers' Association and published by
Which? Ltd, 2 Marylebone Road, London NW1 4DF
Email address: books@which.net

Distributed by The Penguin Group:
Penguin Books Ltd, 27 Wrights Lane, London W8 5TZ

The author and publishers would like to thank the following for their help in the preparation of this book:
Shari Carr, Phil Ermiya, Charles Bonfante, Matthew Burgess, John Sabine, Scott Snowden, Neil Atkinson

Technical consultant: Simon Rowley

First edition October 2000

Copyright © 2000 Which? Ltd

British Library Cataloguing in Publication Data
A catalogue record for this book is available from the British Library

ISBN 0 85202 806 7

For a full list of Which? books, please write to Which? Books, Castlemead,
Gascoyne Way, Hertford X, SG14 1LH or access our web site at www.which.net

Design and illustrations by Joe McAllister
Section 6 designed by Jason Harris, with illustrations by Nigel Edwards
Cover design by Sarah Watson

Text reproduction by Saxon Photolitho, Norwich
Printed and bound in Spain by Bookprint, Barcelona